PRAISE FOR *PEOPLE AND DATA*

'Based on my own decades-long experience working with organizations on removing data-related barriers and building data-driven strategies, I could not agree more with Tom Redman's guidance to put people at the centre. He's onto something massively important here. If you internalize and act on the people-focussed principles he's suggesting, you will no doubt accelerate and amplify your impact on the business.'
Ted Friedman, former Gartner Analyst and industry thought leader

'For any organization to succeed in the 21st century, it needs people and data. Moreover, as Tom Redman explains here, when these two elements unite and when the benefits of data are extended to everyone in the organization you can transform your business. Whether you are a leader, manager or worker or whether you work in HR, Finance, Operations or Marketing, I heartily recommend reading *People and Data*.'
David Green, co-author of *Excellence in People Analytics*, Managing Partner at Insight222 and host of the Digital HR Leaders podcast

'Offers great insights and advice on how organizations can unleash "real people", working together, to solve the data quality problem, once and for all. We could all benefit from Tom Redman's optimism and experience.'
Maria Villar, Head of Enterprise Data Strategy and Transformation, SAP

'*People and Data* is the provocation that many data managers and executives need to spur them into action. Today's world is driven by data, but, as Tom Redman reminds us, if the data is poor (garbage in), then the outcomes are as well (garbage out). Tom's solution for maintaining quality data lies not in technology but in people – how they are organized, what tasks they are given, what culture they create and how they are motivated, promoted and trained. He explores all aspects of building a world-class data organization.'

Theresa Kushner, former Head of Innovation Center, NTT Data, North America

'Tom Redman has a knack for taking the complex world of data and making it simple to understand and improve. What businesses have struggled with for decades is delivered in this next generational approach: data is predominantly a people issue and must be considered a team sport. In this new book, Redman brings solutions that highlight how regular people working together within and across organizations, under the direction of senior leaders, can finally solve this very expensive and seemingly endless enigma and no longer need to stand on the data sidelines.'

Tom Kunz, former Downstream Data Manager, Shell

'An organization's capabilities and results are a product of the quality and engagement of its people and the quality of the organization's systems, structures, processes and culture within which the people work. This book provides pragmatic guidance to address both parts of this equation so you can leverage data as a competitive advantage to achieve your mission.'

Bob Palermo, former Vice President, Performance Excellence, Shell

'An exceptional resource by one of the world's leading thinkers and practitioners on data. Every professional, with data in their title or not, should read Tom Redman's book and learn from his experiences developed over 25 years as the "Data Doc".'

Anne Marie Smith, Alabama Yankee Systems, LLC

'A practical, easy-to-read and anecdote-filled guide for managers embarking on unleashing the power of data within their organization. The book focusses on the often neglected but most important role of people in making data a potent resource for competitive advantage.'

Raghunandan Menon, former Acting Deputy CEO, Gulf Bank, Kuwait

'Nothing of quality happens without quality people, fuelled with quality data, making quality decisions. Here Tom Redman establishes the case, roadmap and tools for dramatic business growth through quality data. "Lead people, manage assets", goes the adage. Tom shows us sensible ways to lead regular people in uniting to success-fully manage the unique assets of data and information technology. Fortune favours the brave – so read *People and Data* and lead bravely for sustained business growth.'

Robert Pautke, Founder and Leadership Coach, SOAR with Purpose, LLC

People and Data

Uniting to transform your business

Thomas C Redman

KoganPage

First published in Great Britain and the United States in 2023 by Kogan Page Limited

2nd Floor, 45 Gee Street
London
EC1V 3RS
United Kingdom

8 W 38th Street, Suite 902
New York, NY 10018
USA

4737/23 Ansari Road
Daryaganj
New Delhi 110002
India

www.koganpage.com

Kogan Page books are printed on paper from sustainable forests.

ISBNs
Hardback   978 1 3986 1087 3
Paperback   978 1 3986 1082 8
Ebook   978 1 3986 1086 6

British Library Cataloguing-in-Publication Data
A CIP record for this book is available from the British Library.

Library of Congress Cataloging-in-Publication Data
Names: Redman, Thomas C., author.
Title: People and data : uniting to transform your business / Thomas C. Redman.
Description: London ; New York, NY : Kogan Page, 2023. | Includes bibliographical references and index.
Identifiers: LCCN 2023013876 (print) | LCCN 2023013877 (ebook) | ISBN 9781398610828 (paperback) | ISBN 9781398610873 (hardback) | ISBN 9781398610866 (ebook)
Subjects: LCSH: Management–Statistical methods. | Organizational effectiveness. | Organizational change.
Classification: LCC HD30.215 .R44 2023 (print) | LCC HD30.215 (ebook) | DDC 658.4/033–dc23/eng/20230406
LC record available at https://lccn.loc.gov/2023013876
LC ebook record available at https://lccn.loc.gov/2023013877

Typeset by Integra Software Services, Pondicherry
Print production managed by Jellyfish
Printed and bound by CPI Group (UK) Ltd, Croydon, CR0 4YY

*For Nancy
and our continuing adventures*

CONTENTS

LIST OF FIGURES AND TABLES

TABLES

FOREWORD

It was 1996, and I had just been assigned a project to improve the 'quality' of my organization's referential data platforms. I soon realized I was ill-prepared for this task, having previously served as an Armor Officer in the US Army, worked in various roles at a small asset management firm, and somehow ended up in financial operations with a goal of achieving something I didn't even know existed – data quality.

I often say that sometimes in life you are smart, and sometimes you are lucky. In the case of my career in analytics it was purely luck and happenstance. A few weeks into the project, I crossed paths with a guy named Tom Redman, who had recently been hired by my company to provide general consulting services on data quality – the topic I knew nothing about. Someone sent me to him, or vice versa.

I assumed that, at our first meeting, this 'data quality' consultant would ask me lots of questions about my data's structure, formats and sources. But Tom didn't talk about any of that. It has been over 25 years since this first meeting with Tom, and I will never forget the simple question that he asked me that day: 'Who is the customer of your data?' I remember thinking that this guy was nuts. Customers are people who pay for products and services. I had never thought of them in this context before. But Tom persisted in his kind yet firm way. By the end of the meeting, while I wouldn't say I was a convert, I was certainly intrigued enough to continue the conversation. I would spend the next year working with Tom. In all truth I felt like I was some sort of modern-day apprentice and he was my master teacher. And along the way, I found that some of the simple techniques that Tom prescribed – process improvement, clear accountability, oversight committees, quality metrics, etc, really worked. And even better, they didn't really cost that much or require massive investments in technology (but you did need an open mind!).

Tom also taught me that data is not just about data – it is about people, how you structure your organization and the processes you implement. It's about creating a horizontal view of your business and breaking down organizational silos. And it's about leadership and culture. But most of all (as Tom reminded me in our first meeting), it's about the 'customer'. Until you 1) sort out who that is, 2) figure out what they need and 3) determine what 'fit for purpose' means for their data needs, you shouldn't spend a dime.

Tom was my first real mentor in this field of data and analytics. And while, of late, people may suggest that I am a thought leader in Generative AI, machine learning and other forms of analytics, I would strongly argue that none of this would be possible without well-defined, high-quality, consistent and accessible data. Tom taught me this 25 years ago, and it has stuck with me ever since.

A few years after I met Tom, I told him that he was probably a few decades ahead of his time in terms of his thinking. I was right about that. Most organizations struggle to understand the value of their data and to holistically address the issues that prevent them from unlocking that value.

Well, congratulations, Tom. The world is catching up with your thinking at just the right time, and your ideas are more relevant in today's data and analytically driven world than ever before.

I hope you enjoy Tom's book and encourage you to experiment with some of the ideas he has shared. That's the other thing Tom taught me – don't worry about getting everything right. Just try different things, learn from your mistakes and move on with the goal of improving your data (and organization) each day.

And most of all, don't ever forget your customer…

Jeff McMillan
Head of Analytics, Data and Innovation
Morgan Stanley Wealth Management
New York City

ACKNOWLEDGEMENTS

Throughout my career, I've been lucky to bump into businesspeople with interesting problems and open minds. We worked together to find novel solutions and apply them in demanding real-world environments. Many great ideas, approaches and techniques, far more general than the original problem, emerged as a result.

Sometimes we ran into organizational issues that held us back. For example, some companies reason that data is in the computer, so if there are quality issues, we should look to our tech departments to solve them. Tech would do the best it could, implementing a tool to point out potential errors. But addressing root causes was beyond Tech's reach, so the problems never went away. These experiences helped me see the importance of getting the organization right: when we did, things moved quickly. And when we didn't, progress came to a screeching and painful halt.

I've also been lucky to bump into great data professionals who shared my interests. We developed underlying foundations, addressed specific issues as they came up, formed study groups to address bigger opportunities, and joined associations to push common agendas. All of this complemented my work on real-world problems.

I've been lucky to bump into terrific editors in professional journals and, later, at *Harvard Business Review* and *Sloan Management Review*. This helped me expose both the successes and the underlying thinking in the demanding court of public opinion. The fear of public ridicule and some terrific editing sharpened my ability to express myself.

Finally, I've been lucky enough to put many of the ideas contained in these pages into practice in the most demanding environment of all – home. From asking 'Who's our most important customer?' to 'Do the facts really support our decision?' to clarifying expectations, to getting everyone involved, many of the ideas expressed here are battle-tested!

To be clear, I've had my share of abject failures. Still, a sort of virtuous learning cycle of trying novel solutions on important problems;

sorting out what worked, what didn't, and why; writing things up; and exposing them at home goes back to the data quality lab at Bell Laboratories and has continued ever since.

The pandemic allowed me an opportunity to resynthesize all I had learned in a disciplined manner. This book is a product of that synthesis.

I've had the pleasure of working with thousands of people and so many have contributed (some admittedly by being downright hostile!). Here are the best of the best.

Business partners Mai AlOwaish, Sabeeka AlRashed, Zahir Balaporia, Sven Berg, Anth Boxshall, Don Carlson, Nikki Chang, Tom Crimmins, Stan Dobbs, Chris Enger, Stephanie Fetchen, Karl Fleischmann, John Fleming, Brian Fuller, Sanda Fuller, Rob Goudey, Matthew Granade, Steve Hassman, Brent Kedzierski, Liz Kirscher, Ken Knowles, Andrei Korobov, Tom Kunz, Jeff McMillan, Raghu Menon, Don Nielsen, Andy Nodine, Roseann Palmeiri, Bob Palermo, Dennis Parton, Bob Pautke, Randy Petit, Grant Robinson, Yekaterina Romanyuk, Kim Russo, Ken Self, Susan Stuntebeck, Bill Sweeney, Shaun Tolchin, Robert Waitman, David Walker, Scott Williamson, Maria Villar and C Lwanga Yonke.

Professional collaborators Salma AlHajjaj, Mary Allen, Bill Barnard, Dave Becker, Alex Borek, Errol Caby, Tom Davenport, Michelle Dennedy, Larry English, Nina Evans, Theos Evgeniou, Mario Faria, Chris Fox, Ted Friedman, Neil Gardner, Blan Godfrey, Brett Gow, Frank Guess, Dave Hay, Roger Hoerl, Young Huh, Rajesh Jugulum, Ron Kenett, Diego Kuonen, Theresa Kushner, John Ladley, Doug Laney, Arnold Lent, Anany Levitin, Danette McGilvray, Tadhg Nagle, Daragh O Brien, Kelle O'Neal, James Price, Andy Redman, Greg Redman, Dave Sammon, Monica Scannapieco, Laura Sebastian-Coleman, Tony Shaw, Anne Marie Smith, Divesh Srivastava, Huzaifa Syed and John Zachman.

Editors, publishers, and writers Lucy Carter, Courtney Cashman, Sarah Cliffe, Amy Gallo, Ally MacDonald, Jacque Murphy, Zexna Opara and Tom Stackpole. Jennifer Daniels is my business manager, doubling as the most demanding editor of all!

My six children and seven grandchildren on the home front.

First, last, always, and everywhere, my bride of almost 47 years, Nancy.

It's been an amazing ride. And we're just getting started!

Introduction

Roots from all over

This book has roots in a dinner cruise in Baltimore Harbour in the mid-1990s. I worked at Bell Labs at the time and my team and I had advised an AT&T group on better ways to verify supplier invoice data. Lots of cold, hard cash was at stake at a time when AT&T was in financial peril. A major milestone had been reached and the Baltimore Harbour event was a celebratory dinner.

I didn't know many people and I wandered around, just trying to strike up conversations. By pure luck, I asked one woman how she felt about the work. She grew serious, looked me straight in the eye and said:

> You know, I've worked for this company for 20 years. And I never felt I had any control over anything. But this was different. I was in control, I did what I thought best. And let me tell you what we achieved.

And she went on to do just that. The excitement in her voice still resonates some 25 years later.

I left AT&T soon after and have plied my trade advising companies, and a few government agencies, on their data and data quality efforts ever since. Time after time, I heard similar reactions from people at companies like Chevron, an EPA in Australia, Morningstar, Morgan Stanley, Shell, and plenty of others: 'This (working with data) is just a way better way to work.' 'Now I don't guess, I know.' 'We've drunk the Kool-Aid. And we're not going back.'

I was slow to pull these threads together. But one day I mentioned it to Roger Hoerl, who had helped lead Six Sigma at GE. 'Oh my gosh Tom,' he exclaimed. 'It was that way at GE as well.' And he had just as many stories as I did.

So many people switched on when they improved data quality and/or used data to solve nagging business problems. Data, and the ability to use it, empowers people!

I use the term 'The Data Generation' to refer to those who seek the facts and use them to make things better. This group includes the woman I met at Baltimore Harbour, people I've quoted above, and those who employed Six Sigma at GE. Recently its ranks have swelled as the day-in, day-out indignities of the pandemic, political misinformation, and challenges in finding a new normal have made concerns about data personal in ways that problems at work do not! Some have joined through concern about big issues such as how many really died from Covid. But more have joined due to their frustrations in getting straightforward answers to questions like, 'Will this vaccine really protect my kids?' and 'Where is the yeast your website promised is in stock and I drove 20 minutes to get?'

There has never been a greater need for people to empower themselves with data in their professional, personal and civic lives. While it is true that the more you know, the more you can do, almost anyone, with just a bit of courage, can make important contributions right now. I'll devote significant space to exploring opportunities to improve data quality, to use 'Small Data' and to make better decisions. Those who pursue these opportunities will improve their team's performance and take back their work lives, relieve stress and reclaim balance. I'm stunned by the sheer number and variety of such opportunities and I'm excited for those who pursue them.

This book also has roots in my ongoing struggles to get people and companies to address data quality. Most are well aware that they have data quality issues and go to enormous lengths to compensate. Many spend half of their workdays dealing with mundane data issues – correcting errors, seeking confirmation for numbers that look suspicious, dealing with differences in data from different systems. Finance professionals spend this time so they can produce reports, sales professionals so they can approach customers, decision-makers so they can make trusted decisions, and data scientists so their algorithms don't blow things up. Bad data is an equal opportunity peril.

It is as if everyone has two components to their jobs: their jobs and dealing with mundane data issues. Like it or not, practically everyone must manage data, an often frustrating job made worse by time pressures and without any formal training on how to do so.

In our business we advise people that there is a better way – don't deal with endless data issues, make them go away. It is stunningly effective, not that difficult, and empowering. We wondered how we could interest more companies in doing so?

Our analysis revealed a key person – someone with a business problem and an open mind to new ways to address it. It was such people who took our advice to heart, made enormous improvements and, in so doing, wrote a script for their organizations. They are charter members of the data generation and so important that we gave them an exalted title, 'provocateurs'. They are the real heroes in the data space.

Once again, it is people that really matter. I don't think any provocateur had data quality as their first interest. Rather, they had a business problem – dealing with invoices, managing risk, proving they were better than a competitor – to solve. Higher-quality data was simply a means to an end.

Its third set of roots lie in the growing importance of data. There have been many success stories and the potential is so great that *The Economist* boldly proclaims that 'data is the new oil'.[1] For many, data may well represent their best chance to improve their businesses and distinguish themselves from their competitors (see the box 'Why all the excitement about data?').

Still, any fair-minded person would agree that progress is agonizingly slow. Some 20 years ago *Harvard Business Review* proclaimed that we've entered 'The Age of Analytics'. Yet today most data is still bad and comes with an enormous price tag. The failure rate of data science projects is way too high, even among great companies with huge quantities of data and deep pools of talent.[2,3,4]

The disconnect between the stunning successes and the many more failures led me to examine 'why is progress so slow?' more carefully. I reached out to dozens of people. I formed study groups to address specific problems. I tried to learn from successful transformations in other contexts. I did my best to recognize my own biases – I am certainly the world's most passionate advocate for data quality specifically and among the top few for all things data more generally.

WHY ALL THE EXCITEMENT ABOUT DATA?

While the specific opportunities vary for each company, team and individual, they include:

1 Every legitimate business effort, from simply delivering your products, to managing the business, to setting strategic priorities, to creating competitive advantage is easier and more effective with better data.

2 Better data reduces cost, often dramatically.

3 Data science yields insights that cannot be obtained in any other way, offering opportunities to better connect with customers and improve products, processes and services.

4 Better data and data science enable better decisions, with all the incumbent benefits.

5 Data creates a myriad of business opportunities. For example, some data earns 'proprietary' status, offering the possibility for sustained advantage.

6 Data fuels advanced technologies, such as artificial intelligence and blockchain. Again, better data means better results.

7 High-quality data and data science are the best ways to push back against misinformation.

8 Data empowers people (I'm most excited about this one).

Pretty impressive for stuff you can't see, taste or feel.

People, people, people!

There are many barriers holding companies back. At the top of the list: 'regular people', those that do not have 'data' in their job titles, are missing from too many data programmes. Companies cannot truly improve quality without them. Nor expect better decisions. Nor expect to implement hard-won insights from data science into practice. Companies simply cannot succeed without them. Those that have data in their titles are certainly important, to the degree that they can engage regular people. Success depends on a large number of people contributing to data quality, conducting their own small data projects, and helping with larger efforts. In short, companies need a large, diverse internal data generation.

Note how empowerment, provocateurs and the data generation work together:

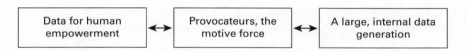

Anyone who doubts the importance of people should read the article 'How humanity gave itself an extra life'.[5] The article says that 'Between 1920 and 2020, the average lifespan doubled. How did we do it? Science mattered – but so did activism.'

People, people, people! Today, in this tech-crazed world, I find something profound, exciting and hopeful in this message. If you take one lesson from this book, let it be 'get everyone involved'. It is why this book is titled *People and Data*. I'll devote significant space to the things companies must do to develop people, point them in the right direction, and unleash them at scale. For many, the subtle shift from seeing people as a part of the problem to seeing them as essential to the solution will prove a tall order.

Management innovation needed

The four other most important (and interrelated) barriers include:

1 Confusion about the proper roles for data and information technology.

2 Organizational silos, which make it more difficult to share data and work across departments.

3 The absence of organization cultures that value data (or alternatively, data-driven decisions or other expressions of this concept).

4 The lack of senior business leadership. Is it any wonder that organizations find it near impossible to replicate hard-fought successes?

Let's dig just a bit deeper.

People and companies don't give data its due, often subordinating data to information technology. It is easy to get seduced by technology – just look at high-flying Apple, Google, Facebook and others. But even the most sophisticated algorithm is no better than the data on which it is based – recall the ravages of 'garbage in, garbage out'! Further, surprisingly to some, in many cases data is already far more valuable than information technology, even as technology garners the larger share of attention.[6,7] The damage that stems from subordinating data to tech is enormous. Even from a narrow technological perspective, when data doesn't get the attention it merits, many otherwise worthwhile tech projects fail.

Data binds a company together. Marketeers develop LEADS data; which is passed onto salespeople; who pass on ORDER data to operations; who pass on PROCESSED ORDERS to inventory management, finance and product development. The data is summarized in MANAGEMENT REPORTS. And so on. Yet the people in all these departments spend enormous time and energy correcting the data received from upstream.

This simple observation reveals much. I've already pointed out that making the errors go away provides a superior approach. But that requires people working together across departmental lines, and silos make it difficult for people to do so. Silos may have been fine in the Industrial Age – after all, division of labour was a key tenet. But they do enormous damage when it comes to data!

Under these circumstances, is it any wonder that companies lack any sort of 'data culture'?

Regular people, even the most ardent members of the data generation, cannot solve these issues. Nor can they train the Board, establish a common language so computers can talk to each other, or decide how the company will compete with data. Only a company's most senior leadership can do these things. Yet by and large, senior management has remained on the side-lines. Regular people can do much on their own. But they will move much faster when senior management becomes fully invested and tackles these issues.

Make no mistake – data is a team sport! And today's organizations stymie the effort. In a nutshell, they are unfit for data.

Building better organizations for data is the overarching theme of this book. To do so, I'll put regular people front and centre of the new organization for data and build other management innovations around them. I'll propose a number of 'fat organizational pipes' as the best means to deal with silos. I'll discuss proper roles for information technology departments vis-à-vis data and I'll propose two non-delegatable tasks for senior leaders. I'll describe some fairly significant changes in the orientation of data programmes. Most important of all, I'll make roles and responsibilities for data explicit, starting with regular people, top-to-bottom and across the organization. These innovations eliminate enormous costs, make it easier to work across silos, set companies up to enjoy the benefits of putting their data to work, and empower people – in short to transform your business! They motivate my subtitle: *Uniting to Transform Your Business*.

I have no illusion that any of this will prove easy. It is just too easy to accept the status quo. As one physician put it:

> … how willing I had become to accept flaws in the data. Even flaws that certainly contribute to worse patient care, inefficiency, dyscoordination, etc, are so commonplace that I had ceased getting worked up about…

As this quote betrays, companies fritter away large quantities of time and money because they don't address data quality correctly. Turning people loose to attack the root issues will begin to unleash them and free up resources to make the needed investments. For many companies, data quality is a great place to start. Indeed, high-quality data is a prerequisite for putting data to work.

Longer term, figuring out how to proceed, the sequence of business problems to attack, dealing with resistance, letting go of long-cherished assumptions, and getting past countless distractions will require some decidedly old-school management discipline – careful planning, persistence, resilience and courage, up and down the organization chart. More than anything, unleashing people and making the innovations called for here will require courage! From those who unleash themselves, from those asked to do new things, from people who already have data in their titles, from managers and senior leaders, and from entire companies.

So, here's the plan

There are 10 chapters, an Epilogue and a Resource Centre. The first chapter is a sort of 'bottom-up' view of data. Though largely invisible to her, data plays key roles in a typical Tuesday for Ann, a 38-year-old marketing executive with two small children. That data is so useful to Ann illustrates the enormous potential. And some of the problems.

It is always important to first understand the problem and the opportunity in detail. The second chapter builds on the first, summarizing my review of the data space: why data is so important and what's gone well, juxtaposed against the enormous people and organizational issues that must be surmounted if companies are to capture the value their data offers. Other chapters dig more deeply into these subjects.

Chapter 3 is a full-spectrum look at a better organization for data. It features a graphical representation of the most essential organizational components and, critically, how they relate to one another. As promised, people, especially the data generation, are at the centre of that graphic. I've seen many organization charts in my day, but never one that puts people at the centre.

Said differently, Chapter 2 explains how organizations are unfit for data and Chapter 3 summarizes what to do about it.

These three chapters make up Part One, 'The Big Picture'. Part Two, 'People', also consists of three chapters, these focussed on people. Chapter 4 presents a stone-cold sober look at the practical realities associated with people joining the data generation. Some people (e.g. provocateurs) empower themselves and show real leadership. Others also empower themselves, but choose not to lead. I am especially excited for these two groups for, as I noted earlier, opportunities abound!

Still other people need a little push – maybe they seek an invitation, some training so they can do the work, or just a reassuring word from the boss. For these people, companies must clarify the new roles and responsibilities that they want people to fill, assign specific tasks and provide some support. Finally, some 'laggards' will choose to remain on the side-lines. I find that most eventually seek different jobs.

Chapter 5 dives into opportunities for both people and companies in data quality. I've already noted that most companies' data is far worse than they imagine, wasting time and money and throwing a wet blanket on everything they want to do. Making matters worse, most companies don't find data quality 'sexy', preferring to concentrate on analytics, artificial intelligence, and other ways to put their data to work. Like it or not, they must deal with quality and most should do so first! The good news is that opportunities abound. And it is the perfect area for companies to turn people loose. Almost all enjoy their new roles as data creators and data customers far more than the old one of dealing with errors. Finally, improving quality saves lots of money and makes other uses of data possible.

Chapter 6 focusses on putting data to work – to develop new insights, find new ways to satisfy customers, make better decisions and create new revenue. There is an unfortunate tendency to view such work as the province of data specialists but this work is going nowhere without regular people. Opportunities abound for the data generation and for companies that fully engage them.

Part Three, 'Data is a Team Sport', consisting of four chapters, addresses the barriers to teamwork I noted above. Chapter 7 is titled 'Fat Organizational Pipes' and it takes on silos, data sharing other organizational barriers. The chapter explores data supply chains, the data science bridge, embedded data managers, common language, and change management as a means to cope.

Chapter 8 looks at the relationships between people, data and technology.

Chapter 9 addresses leadership. There is an old saying that goes, 'All change is bottom-up, all change is top-down.' It reflects the observation that good ideas come into companies through lower levels, as individuals struggle to answer immediate problems. Those that pass muster wind their way up the hierarchy. And aspirationally, senior leaders take them up, driving everyone to adopt those new ideas and practices. From my vantage point, there have been plenty of bottom-up successes and it is time for leadership to do more. In particular, I see two non-delegatable tasks for senior leaders: building the organization called for here, and connecting data and business strategy. Taking these steps will force senior leaders to think deeply about the data cultures they would like to create.

There are a lot of moving parts here. Throughout, the book clarifies management responsibilities for data, pushing them outwards. Much encouragement, training and coordination, as well as a few tasks best done centrally, fall to data teams. Chapter 10 provides a full description of the data teams companies need now.

The Epilogue wraps things up from a historical perspective. It stems from an observation by the famous economist Joseph Schumpeter that world-changing technologies arrive in 'clusters'. Thus, with the printing press came technologies to make ink and paper cheaply and in quantity; and 'content' – books other than Scripture. By this standard, without high-quality data, today's cluster of information technologies is incomplete. Later, historians build on these observations, pointing out the need for organizational innovations to take advantage of the cluster and for people to embrace the technology. While the main purpose is to provide a new framing and urgency to the innovations laid out here, the historical perspective also exposes why exciting technologies such as artificial intelligence are yet to deliver on their considerable potential.

Finally, by and large this is a 'how to think about things' book and I realize that most people learn by doing. No apologies – so much data work has failed because people have not thought deeply enough about what success requires. Still, I want to encourage people to take action – to repeat the force field analysis and the data quality measurement I note in Chapter 2 within their companies, to complete improvement projects, to manage their data supply chains, and to start training people right away. So I've included an extensive Resource Centre that summarizes how to use some of my favourite tools and outlines the training regular people need now.

Notes

1 *The Economist*. The world's most valuable resource is no longer oil, but data, 6 May 2017, www.economist.com/leaders/2017/05/06/the-worlds-most-valuable-resource-is-no-longer-oil-but-data (archived at https://perma.cc/59UA-MXZP)

2 T Nagle, TC Redman and D Sammon. Only 3% of companies' data meets basic quality standards, *Harvard Business Review*, 11 September 2017, hbr.org/2017/09/only-3-of-companies-data-meets-basic-quality-standards (archived at https://perma.cc/52RF-CGVT)

3 TC Redman. Seizing opportunity in data quality, *Sloan Management Review*, 27 November 2017, sloanreview.mit.edu/article/seizing-opportunity-in-data-quality/ (archived at https://perma.cc/CE3A-BP93)

4 Venture Beat. Why do 87% of data science projects never make it into production?, 19 July 2019, venturebeat.com/2019/07/19/why-do-87-of-data-science-projects-never-make-it-into-production/ (archived at https://perma.cc/P4VG-TLUT)

5 S Johnson. How humanity gave itself an extra life, *New York Times Magazine*, 21 July 2021, www.nytimes.com/2021/04/27/magazine/global-life-span.html (archived at https://perma.cc/4BL7-PEZ3)

6 See M Kantor. What is the business value of location data?, Esri, 9 February 2021, www.esri.com/about/newsroom/publications/wherenext/what-is-the-business-value-of-location-data/ (archived at https://perma.cc/DF6K-VY2B)

7 Ocean Tomo estimates that, as of 2020, intangible assets comprise 90% of the value of S&P 500 firms, www.oceantomo.com/intangible-asset-market-value-study/ (archived at https://perma.cc/AVM4-C3AX)

PART ONE

The big picture

1

Ann's data Tuesday

A day in the life

Most people don't give data a second thought. But much like air and water, it is essential to daily life. Consider Ann's Tuesday.

Ann is 38, a market researcher at Upscale Sweater, married to Kelly, and mother to 8-year-old George and 6-year-old Sasha. The four rent a two-bedroom apartment in the city where Ann and Kelly work.

Her day begins at 6.30 am, when Kelly wakes her. They both work at their offices on Tuesdays and he's leaving now so he can put in his day and meet the kids after school. For Ann, the treadmill is first. Thirty minutes at 15 minutes per mile, and a good start to her 10,000 steps-a-day target.

After a quick shower, she wakes the kids, helps them get dressed and feeds them breakfast. It's 'Animal Day' at George's school, so she remembers to lay out his gorilla shirt. And she cuts Sasha's toast diagonally, just the way she likes it. She reminds herself to tell her parents about this – the kids are staying with them Saturday night and she wants Sunday morning to go smoothly. While making their lunches, she makes a mental note that they need more bananas and raspberries. But gosh, raspberries have got so expensive!

Ann puts the kids on their school bus at 8.15 am and heads to the subway for her trip to the office. On the way, she checks the time of her big meeting – 1.00 pm. Ann is in line for a promotion. She is presenting her recommendations for next year's line to senior management, and she needs to be at her very best. She attends two scheduled morning meetings, and the first chance she gets, she opens her 'sales trends' spreadsheet to review the numbers. She wants to make sure she's on solid ground for her main recommendation, starting a new line of light blue sweaters and discontinuing the red. She also calls her colleague Arun, in supplier management. Those light blue sweaters mean Upscale Sweater must source a new kind of dye, and she wants to make sure Arun can get it in the quantities her plan will require.

After her big meeting, in which her recommendation is approved, she and Kelly receive an email from Sasha's teacher, Pete. Sasha's doing well in school, but her last maths test score is low. Pete would like Sasha to see the school's maths tutor, who can determine if special help is in order. Ann doesn't really like the school her kids attend. She replies that she and Kelly will talk about it that evening.

That gets Ann thinking again about her kids' futures. She and Kelly grew up in the city, and like it there. But the rent keeps going up and her friends who've moved to the suburbs tell her the schools are better. She'd never thought they would be able to buy a place, but maybe it's time to consider the towns just outside the city. 'Can we afford it?' she wonders aloud.

Ann is just leaving the office when her boss Stephanie catches her. Stephanie congratulates her on her presentation and tells her she received great feedback from senior leaders. Her promotion is all but assured.

She's now running late so, rather than taking the subway, Ann orders up a ride from Lyft (a North American rideshare service). She reflects on the day on the 20-minute ride home.

After they put their kids to bed, Ann and Kelly discuss their days. They talk about the maths review Pete recommended and a house in the suburbs. They find Sasha's three prior maths tests, and she did well on all of them. They recall that she had not slept well before the last test. Best to keep an eye on the next few tests rather than traumatize Sasha. Ann sends Pete a note, asking that he hold off on the tutor.

Next, they discuss moving to the suburbs and find themselves increasingly excited about the idea. They decide to sign up for some online alerts and to contact some real estate agents in person. Kelly agrees to create a spreadsheet to help sort out what they can afford. A friend had told him about a great online resource. Ann worries about sharing their income online, but sees no alternative.

As they're turning off their lights, Kelly turns to Ann and tells her the following story:

Something interesting happened today. I'm touching up the paint on George's bike and I ran out. You know the hardware store around the corner? I went to their website and checked. They had just what I needed in stock. I took the kids to pick it up, but I couldn't find it. When I asked the guy there, he told me he was sorry, but they were out. He also said that people have trouble with the website every day. Kind of frustrating.

Ann nodded and replied, 'I'm sorry dear. I hope George wasn't too disappointed.' Then she recalls something similar at work:

You know, we ran into a problem like this at work about a month ago. The numbers I need to track sales just didn't look right. I couldn't put my finger on it, so we looked back and found a lot of problems. It took my team most of the week to fix them. And now check the updates every Monday.

Ann kissed Kelly kissed good night and drifted off to sleep.

Note that at no point during her day did Ann say, or even think to herself, 'Let me look at the data' or 'Let me complete this data management task' just as she did not say or even think, 'Let me think about air'. The data is there, but largely invisible.

But data is a big factor in her life. Consider that each of the following (and plenty more) qualify, or could qualify, as data:

- Ann's daily target step count is 10,000
- Sasha likes her toast cut diagonally
- we need raspberries
- big meeting at 1.00 pm
- lighter colours are growing more popular and red less so
- Sasha scored poorly on her last maths test, and
- Ann and Kelly don't know what they can afford to spend on a house

So, what is this data stuff? Why all the fuss? Why, for some, so much excitement? Should Ann care? Should companies?

Data defined

Over the years, hundreds, maybe thousands, of definitions of the word 'data' have been proposed. I like many of them, but the one I like best is the one we settled on some 30 years ago at Bell Labs. In my view, it best corresponds to the way data is created and used in organizations and by people like Ann.[1] It may seem a bit imposing for everyday use, but I find people appreciate it after thinking about it a bit. Using it can help people and companies impose structure, simplify processes, and develop a deeper appreciation for what they know. And don't know!

The basic idea is: The world is bafflingly complex, with all kinds of moving parts, complicated interactions and subtlety. To make sense of it all, we impose structure, using words, concepts and numbers. Someone assigned the term 'raspberry' as the English word for a fruit with certain characteristics (that same fruit is called *framboise* in French and *fu penzi* in Chinese); and Ann and her husband assigned the name 'George' to their first-born.

For data, the structure imposed has two parts: a *data model* and *data values*. Data models define what the data is all about, including specifying things of interest (called 'entities'), important properties of those things (called 'attributes', 'fields', or, in spreadsheets, 'columns') and 'relationships' between them. It is easiest to see this with Ann's sales trends spreadsheet (see Table 1.1).

Spreadsheets are often used to organize data. Each row represents an *entity* (here a week ending on a particular date); each column represents an *attribute* (for example, the number of red V-neck sweaters sold); and the cell provides the associated *data value*. Thus, 5,637 red V-neck sweaters were sold (less returns) in the week ending 12 June 2022.

One can always write a simple sentence such as the one above to fully describe a piece of data (a datum). I sometimes like to employ a shorthand, as follows:

(entity, attribute = value)

TABLE 1.1 Data organized on a spreadsheet

	Number of sweaters sold weekly (less returns)					
	V-neck			Crew Neck		
Week ending	Red	Teal	Light Green	Red	Teal	Light Blue
...						
29-May-22						
5-Jun-22						
12-Jun-22	5,637					
19-Jun-22						
26-Jun-22						
3-Jun-22						
...						

Thus, the cell with the red number in the spreadsheet is written as:

(12 June 2022, red V-neck sweater sales = 5,637)

Now technically speaking, most of the data Ann used is not structured in this way. Rather, it qualifies as 'unstructured data', *statements or observations that have not yet been structured*. Thus, the observations above can be structured. For example:

(Ann, daily target step count = 10,000)

(Sasha, toast cutting preference = diagonally)

(Ann and Kelly, maximum purchase price for house = not yet known)

'Data' is the plural of datum and any collection qualifies. The Upscale Sweater's sales trends spreadsheet that Ann used is a perfect example.

Data everywhere

The simple answer to the question 'Why might Ann care about data?' is because 'it is so darn useful'. Not all data is, but sheer demand for data – which answers questions, makes people's lives easier or more fun, makes employees more effective and efficient, helps everyone make better decisions, leads to new and better products and services – is only growing. Growing demand means opportunity for those that can meet it! Google, Facebook and Uber have reaped great riches by fulfilling demands for data!

Let's review a few vignettes in Ann's day. Even the simplest piece of data (reflecting how Sasha likes her toast sliced) made someone a little happier, and may have prevented a tantrum just before school. And it only took three pieces of data, Sasha's last three test scores, to convince Ann and Kelly to hold off on the tutor, until they got more data!

Ann could not do her job without the sales trend spreadsheet, which integrates data from millions of sales, across hundreds of retail outlets, Upscale Sweater's own websites, and hundreds of sites that sell their sweaters. That data is used for many things, from tracking progress to, in Ann's case, making recommendations for next season's line. Ann could not make these recommendations without the long historical trends it provides.

Complex actions require a broad range of data. For example, Ann could not make her recommendation unless she had data regarding the availability of a special dye. It is not just lots of data, but a complete set of relevant data.

Data may also enable her to see a path to home ownership (see the 'Data wants to be expensive' box). She and Kelly must estimate what they can afford so they can talk to agents. To do so, they'll assemble data about their salaries, their savings and their budget. They'll project new expenses, such as the costs of commuting to the city and possibly a car. They'll estimate savings, such as income tax deductions. Then they'll pull everything together and use an online tool to develop the estimate they need.

Now to repeat, data is still largely invisible to Ann. She can see Sasha's test papers and hears the conversation with Arun. She likes the sleek design of her iPhone, while she is frustrated with the tablet computer she uses at work because it reminds her of system issues. But, while they help her access the data she needs, reach out to Lyft, and complete a host of other tasks, she is more concerned with getting her kids off to school, doing her job, getting Sasha the help she needs, and sorting out the house than she is about data per se. Data just makes successfully completing all those things easier.

> **DATA WANTS TO BE EXPENSIVE BECAUSE IT IS SO VALUABLE**
>
> Many people know the famous Stewart Brand line, 'Information wants to be free', which celebrates how easy it is to share data with modern information technologies.[2] They may be less aware of the first part of the quote, '... that information sort of wants to be expensive because it is so valuable – the right information in the right place just changes your life'. The 'life-changing' helps justify the fuss.

But all is not perfect!

Now, let's dissect Kelly's experience with the hardware store's website and Ann's with company data. For Kelly, wrong data led to a bit of inconvenience for him and a project that remains uncompleted. He still trusts the people in the hardware store, even though he will not use its website again.

The impact of bad data on Ann at Upscale Sweater is far greater. Her team not only had to deal with an initial disaster, but they spend an estimated 10 hours a week running tests and dealing with issues that fall out. That's time they could better spend sorting out a market-ing plan, the job they are paid to do. Worse, decision-makers no longer trust the system and pepper her with questions. In her big presentation, no one questioned her ability to make sound decisions, but they did question the data. Despite their best efforts, Ann herself harbours doubts. If the trend lines weren't so clear, she never would have been able to defend her recommendations!

In some respects, Kelly and Ann are lucky. The bad data could have involved a medical test, putting a family member at risk. At Upscale, bad data could mean bad decisions, lost revenue and fewer jobs.

One other important point about bad data. Malfeasance does not appear to have played a role in either of the examples above. That's not always the case. The unscrupulous use data to mislead – to misstate the condition of a used car, the terms on a loan, the true situation in a political arena. For all the good that data does, Ann and Kelly must be on the alert. Indeed, we must all work very hard to develop a reasonably complete, accurate and relevant collection of data to guide our decisions and actions in any situation.

Greasing the skids of commerce

Now let's look at the data from the perspective of the companies involved. First Upscale Sweater. Much like Ann, data is essential to everything Upscale Sweater does. It uses data to sell sweaters, to run its factories, deliver the right numbers of sweaters to retail outlets, to report to regulators and plan. Without plenty of relevant, highly structured data, Upscale simply could not do business, at profit anyway. Good data means reasonably efficient operations, good decisions and happy customers. Important, but hardly exciting.

But at least some people at Upscale are excited about two things. First, the potential to know more about its customers. Product design people are exploring ways to embed computer chips which detect body heat into the weave and let Upscale know when and where customers are wearing their sweaters. This could be a game changer!

Upscale has also recently hired an advanced analytics team. It is sitting on hoards of data, and this team is charged with figuring out how to utilize it. Yes indeed, Upscale is fully on-board with the hype of artificial intelligence and data monetization and the new revenue streams they could bring.

In part, excitement at Upscale stems from observing Ann's experience with Lyft. Essentially Ann provided two pieces of data: 'I need a ride' and 'here's my location' (more correctly, her iPhone provided her location). Potential drivers provided similar bits of data. Then

Lyft coordinated the ride. Further, with each ride, Lyft adds to its trove of data, fuelling its own analytics to help predict who will need a ride, when and from where and to optimize prices. Pretty simple, or so it seems! And highly disruptive! If Lyft can do it with four pieces of data, imagine the disruption Upscale can cause with all its data!

Next, consider the perspectives of potential lenders. In the not-so-distant past, Ann and Kelly would have filled out a bunch of forms, then met with a banker, who would make a subjective decision as to whether they could be trusted to repay the mortgage. No doubt many bankers were great judges of character. But plenty harboured biases against blacks, immigrants and gay couples and such people suffered. Her parents didn't talk about it much, but they had bad experiences with banks. In ways she didn't fully understand, their experiences had coloured Ann's expectations that she could own a home.

Over time, US Federal law mandated that bias be removed. And slowly, structured data like that provided by independent credit-scoring companies reduced the banker's role, helping to reduce bias; streamline and speed up the process; and reduce costs. Still fintechs such as Rocket Mortgage, seeing the inadequacies of the bank's process, have spotted an opportunity to provide a better service at lower cost. They replaced judgement with algorithms, a much harder task than it may appear. Questions persist about whether known biases have been removed, and whether new ones have replaced the old.

Finally, Neighborhood Hardware. The company knew it had problems with its inventory data. Still, with the owner's knowledge of the store's customers and the help of suppliers who stock the shelves, they manage to have almost everything people want. The website is an embarrassment. But the owner is in a bind – fixing the website didn't seem worth the trouble and taking it down seems like a bad idea. Maybe his friends, who suggest he turn the website into a new way for customers to order, as his larger competitors had done, have the right approach.

Technology amplifies everything

The interrelationships and co-dependencies between data and today's information technologies are many and complex. Most relevant here are the many ways in which information technologies accelerate and amplify the positive and negative impacts of data. Without technology, there is no way that Upscale could pull all its sales data together every week, nor contemplate artificial intelligence. Technology makes it possible for Lyft to find Ann a ride and easier for Pete to communicate with Ann and Kelly. And technology lies at the root of Rocket Mortgage's ability to qualify homeowners for loans almost instantly.

It also allows bad data and its impact to spread more widely and quickly. Even a few years ago, Kelly would not have consulted Neighborhood Hardware's website. He would have called the store and asked about the paint he needed. The person answering would have looked and told Kelly it was out of stock. Neighborhood's inventory system would still be wrong, but the error would not have been exposed to customers. The vignette calls to mind the old saw:

'To err is human. To really foul up, you need a computer.'

But of course, in this case, the root cause isn't bad technology – it is bad data. The computer has just made that bad data more visible.

Technology accelerates and amplifies everything. Magic when it works, greater trouble when it doesn't. Today, social media sites such as Facebook, Twitter and YouTube are front and centre in spreading misinformation, but the problem did not start with them.[3] As Cecil Lewis, a founder of the BBC observed, 'It was quite clear that if you got a madman in front of a microphone, he could do a hell of a lot of damage.'[4] No wonder social media companies earn so much money and wield such power. And garner so much scrutiny.

Most important takeaways

- Data is part and parcel of almost everything we do in our personal and professional lives. Good data makes everything easier and ultimately this explains why all the fuss.

- Most of the time, data is just there – almost invisible and so not garnering the attention it deserves.
- A lot of data is bad, some intentionally so, hurting those who use it.

Notes

1 We developed this definition of data after considering dozens. See C Fox, A Levitin and T Redman. The notion of data and its quality dimensions, *Information Processing and Management*, 30 (1), 9–19. Also T Redman. *Data Driven: Profiting from your most important business asset*, Harvard Business School Press, 2008, which may be easier to find

2 https://en.wikipedia.org/wiki/Information_wants_to_be_free (archived at https://perma.cc/F3M9-KTQ8)

3 J Belluz and J Lavis. Online quackery goes far beyond Seth Rogan, *New York Times*, 11 February 2022

4 Quoted from 'The BBC at 100', *The Economist*, 29 January 2022, 65

2

The opportunity and the problem

The perfect storm

As the vignettes of Chapter 1 illustrate, it is increasingly clear that data offers tremendous advantages to those that manage it professionally and aggressively put it to work.

I strongly suspect this has always been the case. Imagine the data needed to construct the pyramids, administer cities, win wars. Even astrologers needed precise data on the positions of heavenly bodies to do their work. Indeed, one of my favourite articles is titled 'How data became one of the most powerful tools to fight an epidemic'.[1] Interestingly, the epidemic was the cholera epidemic in London during the mid-1800s. The main difference today is that data has invaded every nook and cranny of everything, a trend that, in my view anyway, is only getting started!

In the private sector, data offers companies powerful ways to create competitive advantage, new wealth and jobs, increase productivity, and develop a more empowered workforce. In the public sector, data can help agencies keep us all freer and safer, advance equality, improve public health care, and otherwise improve the human condition. The potential is so great that *The Economist* labels data the new oil.[2] Thus, unlocking this potential could not be more important.

But *doing so* is difficult for even the best, most innovative companies. While there are many reasons, the most glaring is that their organizations are simply not set up for the job – they lack leadership and needed talent at all levels, silos get in the way, and they confuse data and information technologies. In short, they are 'unfit for data'.

Adding to this, while data quality has been a long-standing concern, the pandemic laid bare just how prevalent bad data is and how damaging it can be. For example, managers didn't have the data they needed to navigate the crisis, different groups did not agree on what constitutes a death due to coronavirus, parents wondered for months on end when their kids could return to school. Then many people questioned whether the vaccine was safe and those who concluded that it was wondered when they could get it. To be clear, the pandemic did not exacerbate data quality issues as much as it exposed them for all to see.

This perfect storm of data's growing importance, difficulties in putting it to work, and the ubiquity of bad data leads me to conclude that better managing and utilizing data is THE management challenge of the 21st century.

Some will push back, arguing that implementation of new information technologies such as artificial intelligence, advanced analytics, blockchain, virtual reality and data lakes is the management challenge of the 21st century. There is a forceful argument here. But powerful as these technologies and those in the pipe may be, they are only as good as the data provided to them (the long-time observation 'garbage in, garbage out' has morphed into 'big garbage in, big garbage out'). Further, it is hard to sustain a competitive advantage with technology. After all, your competitors can purchase the same technologies you do. But a company's data is uniquely its own, which means it can become a source of sustained advantage. Confounding the issue, data is not nearly as sexy as the latest new technology, promising riches straight out of the box.

Technology is important. But taken together, these points obscure the central role played by data, and distract leaders. Seen in their proper light, they reinforce the notion that it is data, not information technologies, that represent THE management challenge of the 21st century!

A final note before jumping in. It is easy to see the reach of bad data in the explosion of misinformation and the divisiveness it leads to in our public lives. Interestingly, practically everyone blames social media for accelerating these issues. While my intent is not to make a political statement, first developing a complete, accurate and unbiased view of events may represent THE POLITICAL challenge of the 21st century.

Regular people front and centre

The central thesis of this book is that putting regular people front and centre is the best way for companies to navigate this perfect storm. By a 'regular person', I mean anyone without data in their titles. That includes those on the front line, salespeople, marketing people, new product developers, and those who work in operations and finance, doctors, lawyers and specialists of all kinds. Almost all managers and senior leaders are regular people. In many cases, a company's customers qualify as regular people. The point is to cast a wide net, including everyone who touches data in any way. Importantly, the term 'companies' should be interpreted quite broadly to include for-profit businesses, large and small; government agencies; and non-profits.

The notion that companies should put regular people front and centre is a bold, exciting, and possibly controversial claim, 180 degrees opposite of what most are doing. For example, many promoting digital transformation completely forget about people, or view them as part of the problem. So, I do not make the claim lightly. My goal in this chapter is to summarize the facts as I understand them, my analyses, and how I've reached my conclusions.

Success stories confirm the potential

When I started my career at Bell Labs, statisticians supported all aspects of AT&T business, from product quality, to design and optimization of the network, to business operations. At that time, statistics was largely the province of large companies and government agencies and practitioners immersed themselves in helping solve important business problems.

The success of *Moneyball* by Michael Lewis in 2003, and the subsequent movie, about the small baseball market Oakland A's use of analytics to compete against big money brethren, helped put analytics on the radar screen.[3] Driven by some technological improvements and the hype surrounding data science, more and more companies have started programmes to put their data to work. (NOTE: I cast a wide net in defining data science to include advanced analytics, artificial intelligence, statistics and the like.)

There is plenty of substance behind the hype. Digital natives such as Amazon, Facebook, Google, Netflix, Tesla and Uber recognize the importance of data, the ability to analyse it, and the means to put it to work. Their market capitalizations reflect the value investors place on these points. Uber, perhaps more than any other, illustrates the potential in data. Consider that they have basically figured out how to connect two pieces of data: 'I'm looking for a ride' and 'I'm looking for a fare'.

Data science has gained traction in non-digital natives as well. Indeed, entire books are devoted to examples. It helps UPS save 100 million miles and 10 million gallons of fuel annually; it helps Darden Restaurants improve customer experience and keep them coming back; it is adding to profits for farmers; it is changing the way financial advisors work with their clients; it is improving medical practice; data-driven marketing is now de rigueur; and human resources departments are using analytics to make better hires and identify at-risk employees. This list could go on for a very long time. If you don't see yourself here, perhaps you should look harder – hundreds of news articles and plenty of books confirm this claim.[4]

Still, most of this work is performed by full-time professionals. The notion that regular people could join the fun is not entirely new, however. The control chart, invented by Walter Shewhart in the 1920s for use in Western Electric factories, was designed to be used by line workers, equipped with no more than paper, a pencil and a ruler. Control charts became quite important and popular, boosting quality and productivity in tens of thousands of factories. Six Sigma, invented in the 1980s at Motorola and made part of GE strategy by Jack Welsh in the 1990s, extended the notion that regular people could use data to solve business problems beyond the factory. Today, I use the term 'Small Data' to include control charts, Six Sigma and other basic analytical methods that can be applied by hundreds of millions, perhaps billions, of people with relatively small amounts of data. It is even more relevant today, as companies are loaded with problems perfectly suited to small data.[5]

If you and your company are not already, you must get serious about data, data science and other ways to put data to work and learn to make them part of your future.

I know of fewer success stories in data quality, perhaps because it cannot escape the 'not sexy' label. Still, companies that attack data quality the right way have earned great business results. AT&T saved itself hundreds of millions per year by eliminating the root causes of billing issues; Morgan Stanley improved client data, enabling it to better manage risk; Morningstar improved all aspects of its data products; Shell saved hundreds of millions per year across its business lines; Chevron is better able to manage its upstream business; and Aera Energy's investments in common language and data architecture have helped in hundreds of ways for a full generation.[6] Regular people play the most prominent roles in all.

The most obvious business benefit of improved data quality is reduced expense. Many find this point counter-intuitive. But consider that someone (lots of someones actually) must take the time to correct errors and that costs money. Some errors leak through and dealing with the fallout costs even more. Indeed, for many, dealing with mundane data issues has become so embedded in their jobs that they don't notice.

Still, the bigger though impossible to quantify benefit lies in trust. As one executive expressed it, 'I really do appreciate the savings'. But the ability to run the business is worth far more.

If you are not doing so already, you must also get serious about data quality, learn how to attack it properly, and build it into your business plans. As I'll explain, if you must start with either data science or data quality, you should probably embrace quality first.

A yawning gap

Success stories aside, all is not well in the data space. One does not have to delve in very deeply to confirm this statement – one only has to read the news. Consider data quality. An article in *The Economist* of 27 February 2021 starts thus: 'In a sense, 500,000 is just a very big number. It is not even accurate, given that perhaps 100,000 American deaths from Covid-19 were never counted.'[7] It is a stunning, and scary assessment. Without trusted data, people don't know how to respond, scientists can't make trustable predictions of what will happen, and policy-makers can't chart a way forward. Bad data and its impact is front-page news all too often. A sampling includes:

- 'Misinformation deepens a gap in vaccinations', proclaims a front-page *New York Times* article on 11 March 2021.[8]

- 'To lift ratings, nursing homes shroud neglect' notes that 'Despite years of warnings, the system provided a badly distorted picture of the quality of care at the nation's nursing homes.'[9]

- 'How a lie took wing as the Capitol riot raged' recounts how a claim by a Twitter user with a small following that Antifa or Black Lives Matter was leading the 6 January 2021 attack on the Capitol exploded into the mainstream.[10]

- 'Pandemic is throwing a wrench into credit reports' notes that the number of complaints about bad data doubled in 2020.[11]

- 'Cautionary Tales: Wrong tools cost lives' posits that spreadsheet limitations led to 125,000 additional cases of Covid and 1,500 deaths in England.[12]

Of course, most data quality issues don't make the news. Still, bad data is the norm, adding enormous expense, lowering trust, and adding friction to everything one tries to do with data. In my executive education sessions, I ask attendees to make a data quality (DQ) measurement using the Friday Afternoon Measurement technique. The method focuses on the most important and recent data, returning a score from 0 to 100, the higher the better. It is specifically designed to capture the impact of bad data on the organization's work. Thus, the DQ score reflects the fraction of time that the data is good enough to complete work unimpeded. This is important – there is no hiding the fact that a low data quality score means the organization's work has been compromised!

I also ask attendees how good their data needs to be. Some state things like, 'This data is about money. When it is wrong, heads roll' or 'Our data is from healthcare. When it is wrong, people die.' No one has ever said that their DQ score needs to be anything less than the high 90s.

Over the years executives from a variety of industries and departments have made about 200 such measurements. The average score is 55 and only 3 per cent of the 200 meet the high-90s bogey that managers set for themselves.[13] We've not uncovered any industry or type of data that is significantly better or worse than the others. Importantly, almost all executives are disappointed, stunned, or both. Many spend some time in denial, but most realize that they have a real problem.[14] Poor data quality is an equal opportunity peril.

The consequences, from added work imposed on almost everyone, to the suffocating effects on data science, to the lack of trust it engenders, are enormous. I don't see how companies move forward without trust. For now, take 20 per cent of revenue as a good starting estimate of the associated costs of bad data.[15] Clawing those costs back may well be many companies' best opportunity to improve their bottom lines!

The situation in data science is arguably worse. While big successes and failures make the news, the simple reality is that most data science efforts fail. A 2019 *Venture Beat* report cites a failure rate of 87 per cent;[16] O'Neill puts it at 85 per cent;[17] and my colleague Piyush Malik at greater than 90 per cent.[18] A *Harvard Data Science Review* article, which synthesizes surveys conducted by New Vantage Partners,

McKinsey, *Sloan Management Review*/BCG and Gartner, is broadly supportive. Indeed, despite (or maybe because of the hype) according to a *Sloan Management Review*/BCG survey, only 10 per cent of companies reported significant financial benefits from artificial intelligence (AI) efforts.[19] Further, during the pandemic, when insights were at a premium, none of the hundreds of AI tools built to catch Covid passed muster.[20,21] Indeed, machine learning (ML) may be facing a credibility crisis in medicine.[22,23]

Unfortunately, in many cases data science is doing more harm than good. Concerns about bias in facial recognition systems make front-page news – and rightly so. It could well embed historical biases in ways that make them much harder to untangle.[24] And in *Weapons of Math Destruction* Cathy O'Neill provides example after example, involving students, employment candidates, workers, loan seekers, and patients.[25]

Importantly, it takes a lot to succeed with data science. In many cases, the data is simply not up to task. Perhaps 50–80 per cent of the effort on a typical data science project is spent dealing with the issues, but poor data still imperils most AI efforts.[26,27,28,29] Worse, data scientists seem to be broadly aware of the issues, but don't want to get their hands dirty dealing with them.[30] Finally, even when data scientists are able to develop a solid model, deployment is problematic.[31]

The litany of data woes continues. Consider data breaches, such as the Russian hack of US government agencies that started in May 2020 and wasn't detected for months. The extent of the hack and the damage caused may never be known.[32,33] The sheer numbers of hacks and of sensitive data records stolen are growing rapidly (the reporting of such breaches may also be improving). *Security Magazine* reports nearly 3,000 breaches and 36 billion data records exposed in 2020, up from less than 1,000 as recently as 2014 (Digital Garden).[34,35,36] It appears to me that the problem has lost its ability to shock.

Next, consider privacy. I've personally been guided by an insight of an unknown prognosticator who some 30 years ago advised that 'privacy will be to the Information Age what product safety was to the Industrial Age'. Just as societies came to expect companies to protect consumers by making safe products, so too they would expect companies to protect customers' identities and data.

There is some data suggesting the prognosticator's insight may be right. With a few notable exceptions (e.g. China and Russia), everyone says they consider privacy important. In these parts of the world law and custom limit governments' use of personally identifiable information (PII). Some jurisdictions have adopted laws and regulations which put strict limits on what companies can legally do with PII. The General Data Protection Regulation (Europe) (GDPR), the California Privacy Act, and the Illinois Biometric Information Protection Act are notable examples. Even Facebook is quite public in its calls for new internet legislation. Finally, recent research led by Cisco suggests there is a small but influential group of consumers who've taken action against those whose privacy policies or actions offend.[37] This research suggests opportunity for those who engage with these customers.

On the other hand, there are powerful rebuttals to each of these points:

- Few companies act as though they care much about consumers' privacy. There appears to be considerable advantage in sharing PII, using it in marketing campaigns, identifying possible criminals, etc. It is difficult to even understand most companies' policies.

- While Amazon, WhatsApp and Google fines may seemingly be large, generally enforcement of the law is weak and actual fines are low.[38,39]

- Investors are yet to punish companies for violations. Facebook appeared to be in deep trouble after the 2016 Cambridge Analytica scandal, but its share price continues to grow, unabated.

- In the current political situation in the United States anyway, the chances of legislation with real teeth seems remote.

- Violations of privacy no longer shock most people.

The situation appears broadly similar for other regulatory breaches and security. Citigroup was fined $400 million by the OCC.[40] Equifax also appeared to be in real trouble after the 2017 data breach, and paid a $1.38 billion fine in 2020, $1 billion of which was applied to security upgrades that it probably had to make anyway.[41] As with privacy, capital markets and consumers are proving forgiving.

In the United States, unless your offenses are egregious, you probably have little to worry about in the near term. The situation may be more nuanced in Europe and in other jurisdictions, where citizens place a high value on privacy.

Naturally, companies are not completely blind to the opportunities and issues that data presents. And many have hired chief data and/or chief analytics officers to pull together their data programmes. Again, there are many notable successes. Still overall progress is slow and uncertain. For example, the average tenure of a chief data officer (CDO) is less than two and a half years, and less than half are successful.[42,43] In their article 'Are you asking too much of your chief data officer?' Randy Bean and Tom Davenport clarified just how much work there is to be done.[44,45,46] This helps clarify why it has been so hard for CDOs to get traction. Finally, Gartner Group is advising its clients on CxO 5.0. We certainly would not be up to version 5 (in roughly a dozen years) if the role was enjoying acceptance.[47]

Finally, many companies proudly proclaim that they are managing their data assets and/or are adopting data-driven cultures. Yet Tom Davenport and I suspect that at most 5 per cent of companies just about manage their data effectively, never mind fully put it to work.[48] While I have conducted no formal study, it appears to me that many companies simply attach the 'data-driven' label to whatever they are doing and move on. Thus, there is data-driven cloud storage, data-driven marketing, data-driven customer support, and the like. It is hard to discern any difference between these and cloud storage, marketing and customer support.

Diagnosis

Over the past several years myself and others have grown increasingly concerned about the slow progress and high failure rates cited above. Would companies, rightfully demanding results, put on the brakes and seek growth elsewhere?

With this backdrop, I've made a concerted effort to understand why progress is so slow. I reviewed my clients' and others' successes and failures. I spent many hours with the Chair of a mid-sized media company reviewing how various data scenarios would play out in his company. I talked to dozens, maybe hundreds, of people. I formed and/or participated in study groups that dived deeply into parts of the issue, from the business value of data management to data science, to common language, to change management, to data supply chain management. And I vetted results with other experts, in the public domain, and with clients (I've already cited people in the Acknowledgments).

Starting in the autumn of 2020, I began to synthesize what I had learned (actually re-summarize might be a better description as this was certainly not the first attempt to do so). As data is a very broad topic, I broke the analysis into five smaller areas, chosen because failure to deliver in any one can scuttle an otherwise terrific data programme:[49]

- **Data quality**: Poor quality data adds incredible cost and friction.
- **Putting data to work**: Unless companies put data to work in ways that return value, there is little business benefit. Ways to do so include data science (including AI and ML), exploiting proprietary data, creating data-driven cultures, monetizing data by selling it or building it into products and services, and treating data as assets.
- **Organizational capability**: This refers to the people, structure and culture within the organization that support data programmes. For example, silos can get in the way of data sharing.
- **Technology**: Technological infrastructure will be different for each company, but without the right tools and technologies in place, it will be difficult for companies to scale their data programmes.
- **Defence**: This category encompasses all of the major tasks companies have to do to minimize risk, which includes security, privacy and ethics.

I used Force Field Analysis (FFA), a tool derived from Kurt Lewin's change management model, to analyse and visualize driving forces (those propelling data forward), and restraining forces (those holding it back) and graphically presented them to make these forces clear.[50]

To accelerate progress, you can either enhance the driving forces, add new ones, or mitigate the restraining forces. (NOTE: I recommend FFA to all seeking to advance data in their organizations. See Tool A in the Resource Centre for a full description.)

My five FFAs, which I first exposed widely in August 2021, along with short discussions of each, follow.[51] In each case, the driving forces are depicted below the line pushing up on the factor of interest. By contrast, the restraining forces are depicted as vectors pushing the factor down.

Data quality

As the FFA shows (see Figure 2.1), there are solid driving forces that can help companies improve data quality, but plenty of restraining forces as well. Organizational issues dominate. Quality improves rapidly when all those who use data assume responsibilities as data creators (that is, they create data used by others) and data customers (that is, they use data created by others). Unfortunately, most people don't know about these roles properly. Indeed, many companies assign responsibility for data to their IT departments.

The root causes of many data quality issues experienced in one business unit may begin in another, but silos make them difficult to address. As these forces build up and compound, they can imperil some strategic priorities. For example, bad data quality can severely hamper artificial intelligence programmes and digital transformation.

Putting data to work

As the FFA depicts (Figure 2.2), there are plenty of compelling data science success stories. Data science is enjoying a certain amount of momentum: the number of qualified data scientists is growing, major tech companies (the so-called FAANGs) illustrate what is possible, and other companies are excited by the hype and promise of AI.

But the failures vastly outnumber the successes and restraining forces dominate. The built-in structural animosity between data science teams, which is invested in driving change, and the rest of the

FIGURE 2.1 Quality data

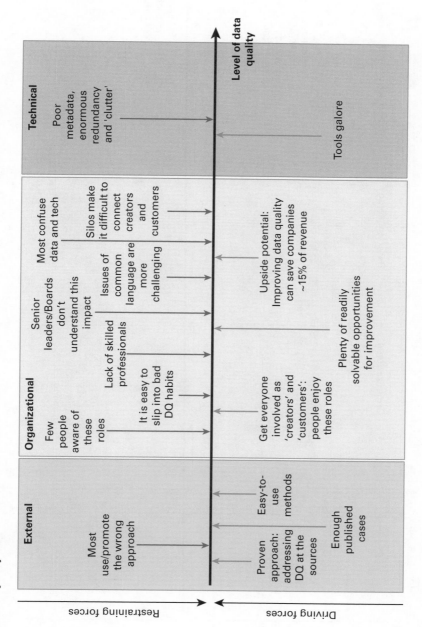

FIGURE 2.2 Monetization/putting data to work

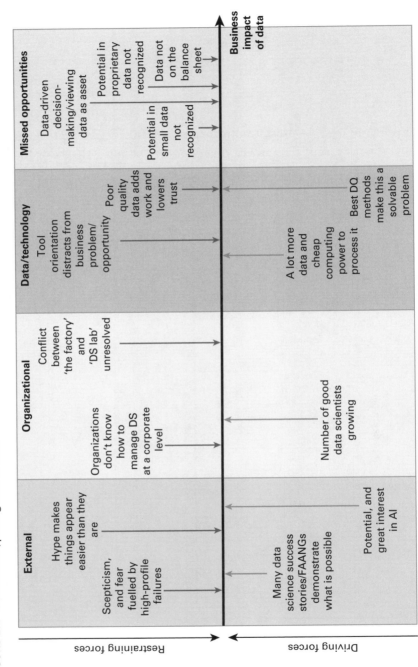

business, which is interested in promoting stability, presents an enormous hurdle. The hype makes data science appear far easier than it is. If it costs a dollar to develop a model, then it costs approximately $100 to deploy it – and companies simply have not made that investment.[52]

Further, data science is only one way to put data to work. Small data, as previously noted, and proprietary data both offer exciting opportunities, but most organizations do not even entertain them. Exacerbating this, data is not on corporate balance sheets or income statements, closing off many potential avenues to monetize data.

Organizational capability

A company's organization is supposed to make it easier for people do their work. But the organization is the major issue when it comes to data, as the sheer number of restraining forces underscores (Figure 2.3). I've already cited three restraining forces – the confusion about the management of data and technology, silos, and people not understanding their roles as data customers and data creators. Four further restraining forces merit special mention.

First, the lack of skilled data architects, engineers and quality professionals makes it more difficult to address the quality issues cited earlier.

Second, while many opine that data is the new oil, preach that data is an asset, or urge their people to make data-driven decisions, the reality is quite different – for most people data is just like another thing they need to do their jobs. Companies do not sort out ways to profit from their data, take care of it, or teach people how to use it to make better decisions. Hype aside, they do not value data.

Third, fear exacerbates restraining forces. Even as individuals don't value data per se, they see and hear all the hype. And they can sort out, in their own minds, that massive change is on the way. People are smart to be scared – that they will lose their jobs, be left behind, lose status, and so forth. Fear also freezes companies, keeping them from making changes they know they need to make.

FIGURE 2.3 Organization

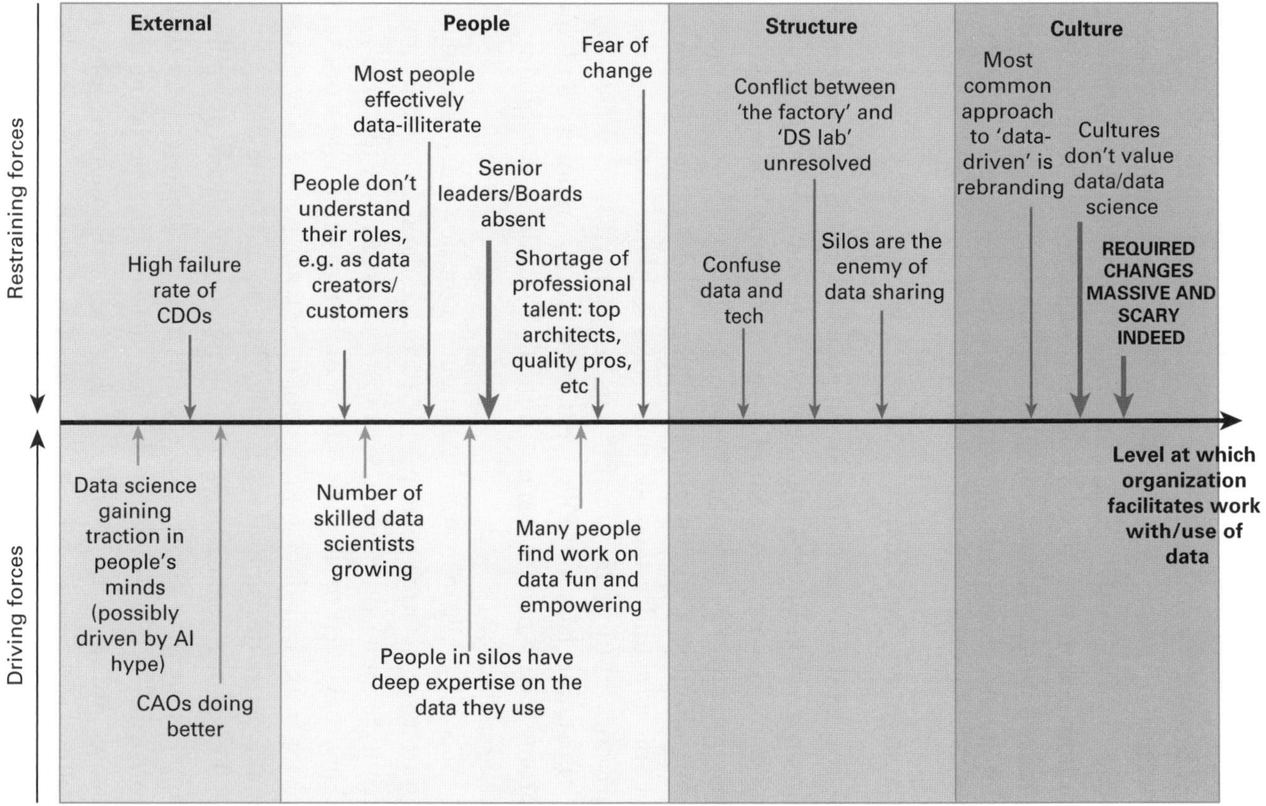

External	People	Structure	Culture

Restraining forces →

High failure rate of CDOs	Most people effectively data-illiterate	Conflict between 'the factory' and 'DS lab' unresolved	Most common approach to 'data-driven' is rebranding
	Senior leaders/Boards absent		Cultures don't value data/data science
	Fear of change		
	People don't understand their roles, e.g. as data creators/ customers	Silos are the enemy of data sharing	**REQUIRED CHANGES MASSIVE AND SCARY INDEED**
	Shortage of professional talent: top architects, quality pros, etc	Confuse data and tech	

→ **Level at which organization facilitates work with/use of data**

← **Driving forces**

Data science gaining traction in people's minds (possibly driven by AI hype)	Number of skilled data scientists growing		
CAOs doing better	Many people find work on data fun and empowering		
	People in silos have deep expertise on the data they use		

Finally, most senior leaders are sitting on the side-lines, perhaps fearful themselves or unsure what to do.

Technology

Many new technologies, including AI, cloud computing and connected devices (the Internet of Things), have proven they can be valuable. Still, implementing new technologies is not easy for most companies, as powerful restraining forces get in the way (Figure 2.4). Technical debt in various guises is a major issue, as are the low levels of data quality cited above.

Perhaps the most serious issue involves poor relations between business and tech people. Many businesspeople readily admit that they don't trust their information technology counterparts; and tech professionals, for their part, report they feel over-worked and under-appreciated. It is difficult to see how companies can take full advantage of the technologies available to them under these circumstances.[53]

Defence

Many forces, such as GDPR and other regulations, a few spectacular fines, the rising spectre of data piracy and malware, and the actions of a few desirable customers, suggest the need for better defence (Figure 2.5). But these forces are generally weak. Further, investors and customers have largely forgiven those who have violated regulations. Still, companies should pay careful attention because the environment could change rapidly.

Summary

To be clear, there is plenty of good news. The basics of data science and data quality have been worked out and are proven. Many technologies are up-to-task and the number of solid data scientists is growing. Still, progress is delayed because today's organizations are

FIGURE 2.4 Technology

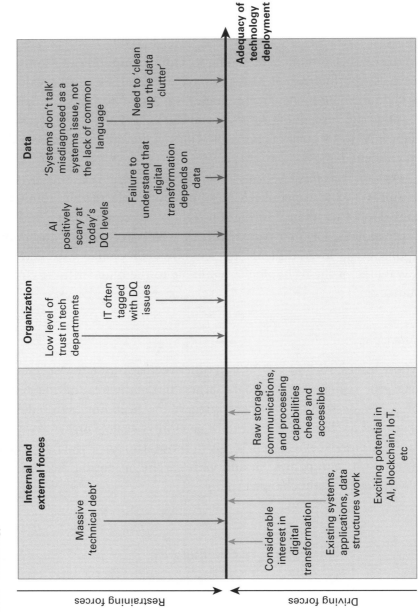

FIGURE 2.5 Defence

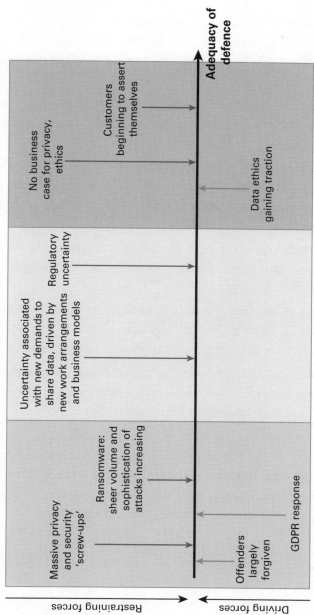

unfit for data, and the obstacles this presents are many and varied. Digging deeper, the seven most important observations include:

1 The most important restraining force is that regular people are missing from data programmes. Companies don't know what they should expect of them and so regular people are left in the dark as to what they should do.

2 Poor quality data has a suffocating effect on day-to-day work, data science and other ways to monetize data, and on implementing new technologies.

3 Silos get in the way. They hinder data quality and interfere with data sharing at all levels. There is considerable tension between data science and business teams. Systems don't talk due to the lack of common language.

4 Most individuals and companies confuse the management of data and the management of technology, hindering proper management of both.

5 Cultures don't value data and data science (even though many say they do). Instead, there is considerable fear of both. This makes a certain amount of sense – the required changes are massive.

6 While companies lack needed talent at all levels, the most important gap is at senior levels. Senior business managers are yet to engage, possibly because they also don't know what they should do.

7 Even as there are a growing number of data breaches and concern for privacy grows, the investment community and general public are yet to seriously punish companies for breaches and privacy violations. Still, uncertainty rules and companies should remain vigilant for changing customer sentiment and regulation.

Given all these issues, one might wonder if companies shouldn't proceed with extreme caution: stay out of trouble by following the law; wait for the approaches, methods and technologies to mature; keep a watchful eye and jump in when the time is right. But this diagnosis confirms that such thinking is short-sighted! Rather, it is organizational issues that hold companies back and waiting will not resolve them. It will take lots of hard work to do so, but they are resolvable.

> In the hands of the open-minded and the skilled, the approaches, methods and technologies are more than up to the task.

The remainder of this book considers the first six of these observations. Broadly, Point 1 calls for getting everyone involved and Points 2 to 6 for fully enacting the 'data is a team sport' mantra.

Most important takeaways

- Data has proven itself time and again. But companies have yet to take advantage of the value it offers. Worse, quality is low and adds enormous friction and risk.
- Today's organizations are unfit for data. The single most important problem is that regular people are not included in the effort.
- Other big issues include: silos and lack of common language keep people from working together; leadership is absent; there is considerable confusion about the roles of data versus information technology; and cultures don't value data.

Notes

1 S Johnson. How data became one of the most powerful tools to fight an epidemic, *The New York Times Magazine*, 10 June 2020, www.nytimes.com/interactive/2020/06/10/magazine/covid-data.html (archived at https://perma.cc/2BX3-HF8P)

2 *The Economist*. The world's most valuable resource is no longer oil, but data, 6 May 2017, www.economist.com/leaders/2017/05/06/the-worlds-most-valuable-resource-is-no-longer-oil-but-data (archived at https://perma.cc/B55G-QB5T)

3 M Lewis (2004) *Moneyball: The art of winning an unfair game*, 1st edn, WW Norton & Company

4 Good places to start are: T Davenport and J Harris (2007) *Competing on Analytics*, Harvard Business Review Press; DB Laney (2018) *Infonomics: How to monetize, manage and measure information as an asset for competitive advantage*, Bibliomotion Inc; DB Laney (2022) *Data Juice: 101 ways to squeeze value from your (and others') data*, Douglas B Laney

5 R Hoerl and T Redman. Most analytics projects don't require much data, *Harvard Business Review*, 3 October 2019

6 TC Redman. Seizing opportunity in data quality, *MIT Sloan Management Review*, 27 November 2017; TC Redman (2019) *Getting in Front on Data: Who does what*, Technics Publications

7 *The Economist*. Now America has passed 500,000 deaths, what next?, 27 February 2021, www.economist.com/united-states/2021/02/25/now-america-has-passed-500000-deaths-what-next (archived at https://perma.cc/85DZ-WAUE)

8 S Frankel. Misinformation deepens a gap in vaccinations, *New York Times*, 11 March 2021

9 J Sliver-Greenberg and R Gebeloff. Maggots, rape and yet five stars: how US ratings of nursing homes mislead the public, *The New York Times*, 14 March 2021, www.nytimes.com/2021/03/13/business/nursing-homes-ratings-medicare-covid.html (archived at https://perma.cc/7G4X-DA4Y)

10 *The New York Times*. How pro-Trump forces pushed a lie about antifa at the capitol riot, 1 March 2021, www.nytimes.com/2021/03/01/us/politics/antifa-conspiracy-capitol-riot.html (archived at https://perma.cc/57SX-FTS3)

11 A Cairns. More consumers complain about errors on their credit reports, *The New York Times*, 20 February 2021, www.nytimes.com/2021/02/19/your-money/credit-report-errors.html (archived at https://perma.cc/L25D-5YQW)

12 T Harford. Cautionary tales: Wrong tools cost lives [blog] 21 May 2021, timharford.com/2021/05/cautionary-tales-wrong-tools-cost-lives/ (archived at https://perma.cc/U265-M3MB)

13 For a full discussion of the Friday Afternoon Measurement method and results of the first 95 measurements, see 'Only 3% of companies data meets basic quality standards', by T Nagle, T Redman and D Sammon, *Harvard Business Review*, September 2017, hbr.org/2017/09/only-3-of-companies-data-meets-basic-quality-standards (archived at https://perma.cc/89S9-ZZLG). That result is little changed since.

14 T Nagle, T Redman and D Sammon. Waking up to data quality, *The European Business Review*, 12 May 2018, www.europeanbusinessreview.com/waking-up-to-data-quality/ (archived at https://perma.cc/KBN6-3WHN)

15 TC Redman. Seizing opportunity in data quality, *MIT Sloan Management Review*, 27 November 2017, sloanreview.mit.edu/article/seizing-opportunity-in-data-quality/ (archived at https://perma.cc/KS3F-SN6V)

16 BT O'Neill. Why do 87% of data science projects fail to make it into production, Venture Beat, July 2019

17 BT O'Neill. Failure rates for analytics, AI, and big data projects = 85% – Yikes!, Designing for Analytics, 23 July 2019, designingforanalytics.com/resources/failure-rates-for-analytics-bi-iot-and-big-data-projects-85-yikes/ (archived at https://perma.cc/8GZV-9YH6)

18 Piyush Malik, personal communication, September 2022

19 T Davenport and K Malone. Deployment as a critical business data science discipline, *Harvard Data Science Review*, 3.1, 10 February 2021, hdsr.mitpress.mit.edu/pub/2fu65ujf/release/2 (archived at https://perma.cc/36EQ-6YXT)

20 WD Heaven. Hundreds of AI tools have been built to catch Covid. None of them has helped, *MIT Technology Review*, 30 July 2021, www.technologyreview.com/2021/07/30/1030329/machine-learning-ai-failed-covid-hospital-diagnosis-pandemic/ (archived at https://perma.cc/R7LK-6NKT)

21 For an analysis of why AI tools failed, see also B Chakravorti. Why AI failed to live up to its potential during the pandemic, *Harvard Business Review*, 17 March 2022, hbr.org/2022/03/why-ai-failed-to-live-up-to-its-potential-during-the-pandemic (archived at https://perma.cc/DFW9-T7ET)

22 For example (see also note 23): R Thomas. Medicine's machine learning problem, *Boston Review*, 19 October 2020, bostonreview.net/articles/rachel-thomas-medicines-machine-learning-problem/ (archived at https://perma.cc/K9D5-CZ8K)

23 C Ross. Machine learning is booming in medicine. It is also facing a credibility crisis, STATNews, 2 June 2021, www.statnews.com/2021/06/02/machine-learning-ai-methodology-research-flaws/ (archived at https://perma.cc/L5D8-A7CW)

24 There are hundreds of articles, and considerable controversy on this subject. I don't have any idea how it will turn out, but I suspect that it will be decades, if ever, before AI is trusted in many applications

25 C O'Neil (2016) *Weapons of Math Destruction*, Crown Publishing Group, New York, NY

26 For example (see also note 27): Alation state of data culture report reveals barriers in adopting artificial intelligence, Businesswire, 24 May 2021, www.businesswire.com/news/home/20210324005134/en/Alation-State-of-Data-Culture-Report-Reveals-Barriers-in-Adopting-Artificial-Intelligence (archived at https://perma.cc/VUW6-DWMU)

27 B Schmarzo. Why data management is today's most important business discipline, Data Science Central, 8 February 2022, www.datasciencecentral. com/why-data-management-is-todays-most-important-business-discipline/ (archived at https://perma.cc/3BBK-55XE)

28 Just a few years ago a Crowdflower study suggested that about 80% of a data scientist's time is spent on data preparation (see also note 29). visit.figure-eight. com/rs/416-ZBE-142/images/CrowdFlower_DataScienceReport_2016.pdf (archived at https://perma.cc/4H9A-WY62)

29 Other surveys have come in with lower estimates (I don't recall seeing anything less than 45%) and others have raised questions about just what counts as preparation (e.g. L Dodds). Personally, I suspect that the fraction is way too high, that there is considerable variation, and that the effort doesn't always go well, posing unknown risk. blog.ldodds.com/2020/01/31/do-data-scientists-spend-80-of-their-time-cleaning-data-turns-out-no/ (archived at https://perma. cc/89R4-RQ46)

30 N Sambasivan, S Kapania, H Highfill, D Akrong, P Paritosh and L Aroyo. 'Everyone wants to do the model work, not the data work': Data Cascades in High-Stakes AI, Google Research Report, 2021, research.google/pubs/ pub49953/ (archived at https://perma.cc/N8JA-MTDZ)

31 T Davenport and K Malone. Deployment as a critical business data science discipline, *Harvard Data Science Review*, 3.1, 10 February 2021, hdsr.mitpress. mit.edu/pub/2fu65ujf/release/2 (archived at https://perma.cc/7V4M-Q6WV)

32 For example (see also note 32): S Shead. Suspected Russian hack is much worse than first feared: Here's what you need to know, CNBC, 18 December 2020, www.cnbc.com/2020/12/18/suspected-russian-hack-on-us-is-much-worse-than-first-feared.html (archived at https://perma.cc/6ZGB-FRCF)

33 DE Sanger, N Perlroth and E Schmitt. Scope of Russian hacking becomes clear: Multiple US agencies were hit, *The New York Times*, 14 December 2020, updated 9 September 2021, www.nytimes.com/2020/12/14/us/politics/ russia-hack-nsa-homeland-security-pentagon.html (archived at https://perma. cc/E2JR-3SQY)

34 One can find rich troves of information on data breaches with simple searches. Here I especially relied on the following (see also notes 34 and 35): M Henriquez. The top 10 data breaches of 2020, *Security Magazine*, 3 December 2020, www. securitymagazine.com/articles/94076-the-top-10-data-breaches-of-2020 (archived at https://perma.cc/C6WP-E7NK)

35 J De Groot. The history of data breaches, Digital Guardian, 22 August 2022, digitalguardian.com/blog/history-data-breaches (archived at https://perma.cc/ PHW9-5TRH)

36 S Shead. Suspected Russian hack is much worse than feared: Here's what you need to know, CNBC, 19 December 2020, www.cnbc.com/2020/12/18/ suspected-russian-hack-on-us-is-much-worse-than-first-feared.html (archived at https://perma.cc/H9ZV-QUAW)

37 T Redman and R Waitman. Do you care about privacy as much as your customers do? *Harvard Business Review*, 28 January 2020, hbr.org/2020/01/do-you-care-about-privacy-as-much-as-your-customers-do (archived at https://perma.cc/F7X8-UBCD)

38 22 Biggest GDPR Fines of 2019, 2020, and 2021 (So Far), Tessian, 19 November 2021, www.tessian.com/blog/biggest-gdpr-fines-2020/ (archived at https://perma.cc/7JJH-U2Q9)

39 *The Economist*. Digital Overreach, 3 September 2022, 47

40 M Volkov. Citigroup fined $400M by banking regulators for risk and compliance control deficiencies, JD Supra, 1 December 2020, www.jdsupra.com/legalnews/citigroup-fined-400-million-by-banking-69177/ (archived at https://perma.cc/BQ2W-JBXV)

41 *Security Magazine*. Lessons learned from the Equifax data breach, 8 September 2020, www.securitymagazine.com/articles/93282-lessons-learned-from-the-equifax-data-breach (archived at https://perma.cc/W752-S2S3)

42 T Davenport, R Bean and J King. Why do chief data officers have such short tenures?, *Harvard Business Review*, 18 August 2021, hbr.org/2021/08/why-do-chief-data-officers-have-such-short-tenures (archived at https://perma.cc/X8CA-HYBS)

43 R Bean. Chief data officers struggle to make a business impact, Forbes CIO Network, 24 June 2019

44 References include (see also notes 43 and 44): *Forbes Insight*. Rethinking the roles of chief data officer, 22 May 2019, www.forbes.com/sites/insights-intelai/2019/05/22/rethinking-the-role-of-chief-data-officer/?sh=66bbc2da1bf9 (archived at https://perma.cc/XPX8-HUDK)

45 J Bennett. Why only half of CDOs are poised for success, Gartner, 11 April 2016, www.gartner.com/smarterwithgartner/half-of-cdos-succeed/ (archived at https://perma.cc/JM9F-MQUE)

46 R Bean and T Davenport. Are you asking too much of your chief data officer?, *Harvard Business Review*, 7 February 2020, hbr.org/2020/02/are-you-asking-too-much-of-your-chief-data-officer (archived at https://perma.cc/MHR4-ATT5)

47 Gartner. Gartner Research Board identifies the CxO 5.0, a new operating model for data, analytics, and digital leaders, 28 April 2022, www.gartner.com/en/newsroom/press-releases/04-28-2022-gartner-research-board-identifies-the-cxo-50-a-new-operating-model-for-data-analytics-and-digital-leaders (archived at https://perma.cc/D76H-6CZ6)

48 T Davenport and T Redman. Getting serious about data and data science, *MIT Sloan Management Review*, 28 September 2020, sloanreview.mit.edu/article/getting-serious-about-data-and-data-science/ (archived at https://perma.cc/5DWM-RV6Q)

49 TC Redman. 5 ways your data strategy can fail, *Harvard Business Review*, 11 October 2018, hbr.org/2018/10/5-ways-your-data-strategy-can-fail (archived at https://perma.cc/AN23-KT4V)

50 K Lewin (1951) *Field Theory in Social Science*, Harper and Row

51 TC Redman. What's holding your data program back? *Sloan Management Review*, 2 August 2021, sloanreview.mit.edu/article/whats-holding-your-data-program-back/ (archived at https://perma.cc/GTA5-YCRA)

52 T Davenport and TC Redman. Getting serious about data and data science, *MIT Sloan Management Review*, 28 September 2020, sloanreview.mit.edu/article/getting-serious-about-data-and-data-science/ (archived at https://perma.cc/5669-EPBP)

53 TC Redman. The trust problem that slows digital transformation, *Sloan Management Review*, 26 July 2022, sloanreview.mit.edu/article/the-trust-problem-that-slows-digital-transformation/ (archived at https://perma.cc/4BUM-ZMES)

3

Building a better organization for data

Building a company suited to addressing the issues described in Chapter 2 requires a different kind of 'organization for data'. A highly federated organization, overlain on the existing organization chart, that places regular people front and centre and provides structures that make it easier for people to work together. One that assigns new roles to data teams to help them be effective and ensures that information technology departments play their appropriate roles. Finally, one that gets senior leadership working on tasks they can actually accomplish and so lead the effort. This chapter introduces the organization needed to achieve this.[1]

Figure 3.1 illustrates the components needed to build an organization more suited for data. This chapter will go into further detail regarding the following components:

- regular people
- fat organizational pipes
- information technologists
- data teams
- leadership

FIGURE 3.1 Components of a better organization for data

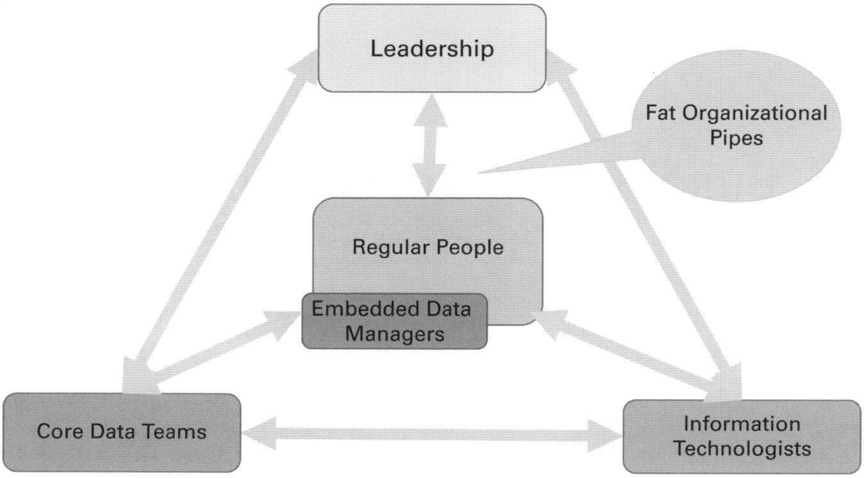

Put regular people front and centre

Missing regular people (as defined in Chapter 2) is the single most important force holding data programmes back. Upon hearing this notion, most people readily agree, admitting they hadn't thought of it and that it is an important insight. After all, if data is to be truly transformational and achieve its potential, companies have to get everyone involved. This is straight out of any 'Management Transformation 101' class.[2] And on a moment's reflection they further recognize that, unintentionally perhaps, people have been excluded.

Benefits

Further, and as more fully explained throughout, regular people are central to all data-related work – from using data in their jobs, to improving data quality, to using data to make better decisions, to embracing a newly developed AI model as a means to improve their work processes. Going one step further, all actual benefits, including increased revenue, decreased cost, lowered risk and closer connections with customers, accrue when regular people use more and better data to improve what they do. Perhaps anticipating this reality, in the early 1950s Samuel Wilks, paraphrasing H G Wells, noted that 'Statistical thinking will one day be as necessary for efficient citizenship as the ability to read and write.'[3] While Wells was talking about people's roles as citizens, not workers, his argument is no less imperative for businesses today.

Succinctly, a company can't do much with its data without getting as many people as it can fully onboard. Without large numbers of people engaged in the data programme, poor results, even outright failure, is highly probable.

These observations explain why regular people are at the centre of Figure 3.1.

Yet today, too many companies view people as 'part of the problem'. As Riona Rooplal, studying digital transformation as part of her master's degree work, put it, 'Everyone thinks about people last, when it is too late to engage them.'[4] Even worse, in a time when many employees are beyond burnt out, they must deal with mundane data issues simply to do their jobs.[5] Rather than seeking new ways to put data to work, many spend half, even more, of their workday correcting errors, seeking confirmation for numbers that look suspicious, dealing with differences in data from different systems.[6] As noted in the Introduction, it is as if everyone's job has two components:

- their jobs
- dealing with mundane data issues so they can do their jobs

It is a huge waste of talent.

Adding insult to injury, many people also fear that statistics, data science, artificial intelligence and/or digital transformation will displace them. It is no wonder they are burnt out.

It is also a huge waste of money and time. Even leaders who don't give a fig about empowerment, employee job satisfaction or cross-silo partnerships must care about productivity.

Data as human empowerment

Over the years I've seen (and often helped) thousands of regular people use data to solve important problems. Many were sceptical, even fearful, early on. But as they got into it, the vast majority found they enjoyed the work, loved the personal growth, and took great pride in their contributions. These contributions ranged from uncovering, then eliminating, the root cause of a quality problem, discovering simple ways to improve their team's performance, or helping sort out how to build a new analytic technique into their work.[7,8] They enjoyed the teamwork, especially working across silos and company boundaries. Many who had suggested improvements before – when equipped with data – could prove their cases to management. This proved especially sweet!

My best analogy to the excitement people find in learning new data skills is the glee youngsters feel when they learn to ride a bicycle. They are so proud of themselves! And they soon find that riding a bike gives them freedoms they just didn't have before. So too with data. As one mid-level manager expressed, 'We've seen the light. And we're not going back!'[9] This manager and the woman in the first vignette of this book, excited to finally have some control, are all too typical. People at all levels, in industries as diverse as consumer products, energy, finance and healthcare, have experienced these pleasures. To the surprise of many, so too have unionized employees. And an engaged, excited workforce is a productive workforce.[10]

To complete the case for seeing data as human empowerment, companies are loaded with problems that teams of regular people, with small amounts of encouragement and training, can solve. Regular people have so much to contribute. Opportunity abounds, for individuals and companies courageous enough to seize it. Help people empower themselves with data and good things follow!

Observations

These simple observations are really important. They mean that every data science project should start with the question, 'Who might be impacted and how do we get them involved?' Every effort to address data quality must start with the question, 'Who touches that data and how do we get them involved?' Every effort to improve business performance must start with the question, 'What data do we need to complete this effort and who do we need to get involved?' And every company-wide data programme should start with, 'How do we get everyone involved?'

It is a subtle, yet profound, change in thinking. People and companies must employ a variety of tactics to get people involved. Fortunately, many regular people are ready to sign on.

Responsibilities, not just rights

Of course, if companies want their people to contribute, they must figure out what they expect of people, explain it to them, and provide guidance, training and support. I see five major areas where regular people can, and eventually must, contribute:[11,12,13,14,15,16]

1 as *customers* and *creators* in **quality programmes**

2 as *small data scientists* in **process improvement**

3 as *collaborators, customers* and *data creators* in **larger data science,** artificial intelligence, digital transformation, and other monetization projects

4 as *guardians* of the company's data assets, especially in understanding and following **privacy and security** policy

5 as better *decision-makers*

DATA CITIZENSHIP

The notion of data democratization, or data citizenship, has gained a certain amount of attention recently. The basic idea is that people have rights to access, trust and share ownership for data. It is an important idea and I am all for it.

But it doesn't go far enough. For there are no rights without the means to secure them and clear responsibilities. Similarly for data – a big part of putting people front and centre involves clarifying exactly how you expect them to contribute.

As regular people take on these roles, they join the Data Generation, a group I noted in the Introduction and will discuss more fully in Chapter 4.

Of course, few people will divine these expectations on their own, nor know where to focus. Companies must first think long and hard about what they want to achieve with data. As I'll explain in Chapters 5 and 6, most should start with quality, followed by small data. Imagine the powerhouse if instead of those above, the two components of everyone's job were:

- their jobs
- helping improve their team's performance and the performance of teams elsewhere in the company

The transition can occur in two steps, as Figure 3.2 depicts. Data makes this possible. Properly unleashed, it empowers people AND entire companies!

As they grow comfortable in attacking data quality and in small data, companies will face some hard, strategic choices. Does the long-term strategy depend on artificial intelligence, proprietary data, small data, better decisions, something else? Which business opportunities will go first and drive the data programme? What parts of the effort will be centrally, or locally, driven? How will the company achieve and sustain some competitive advantage? How aggressively does the company wish to pursue privacy and security? These questions can only be answered by a company's most senior leaders, with the assistance of full-time data professionals. I'll discuss these topics in Chapter 9. But whatever the answers, it is almost certain that regular people must be front and centre.

FIGURE 3.2 Proposed transition of regular people's job via data quality and small data projects

Fat organizational pipes

Specialization, division of labour, the factory assembly line, and the hierarchical form are among the great management innovations of the Industrial Age, facilitating the huge expansions in capacity that came with that period. These ideas were so successful that they pushed outward from the factory to the back office and distribution channels.

Today, they are a mixed blessing. I've noted that data flows across departments in a sort of daisy chain: leads data is needed to develop ORDERS, PROCESSED ORDERS, MANAGEMENT REPORTS, and so on. Everyone is using data to do their jobs and in turn passing on data they create to the next person in line.

In an Industrial Age factory, the assembly line provided the coordination necessary to build a car. One team installed the engine, another hung the doors, a third painted the car, and so forth. And people hanging doors didn't have to think about paint! They certainly didn't have to waste time touching up a bad paint job, unlike today's salesperson who spends considerable time fixing up data from the marketing department.

Exacerbating these issues has been the balkanization of the IT systems used by each department. Thus marketing, sales, finance, operations and management all have their own systems, some of which 'talk together' well, but most less easily. The impact has been to increase technical debt and to make organizational silos higher and thicker.

Seen in its proper light, data is a team sport, requiring unprecedented coordination among regular people. I've coined the term 'fat organizational pipes' as the means to provide this coordination. The customer–supplier model, data supply chains, common language, the data science bridge, and proactive change management, each tailored to fit specific needs, provide such. I'll discuss them in greater detail in Chapter 7. Importantly, data teams must play a large role in setting up and maintaining these pipes.

Separate the management of data from the management of information technology

Great data programmes deserve great information technology. But today, the gap between what companies get and what is possible is large and growing. From my perspective, both 'the business' and information technologists contribute to the gap. The issues start with confusion about the proper roles of data versus the information technologies that help create, store, transport and process the data. In particular, too many people conflate the two, or worse, subordinate data to tech. An unhealthy dynamic ensues in which the business develops unrealistic expectations of its IT department, which then fails to deliver, reducing business's trust in IT. Information technologists could push back, demanding that the business hold up its end, but rarely do. And an uneasy stasis, in which tech is viewed poorly, morale is low, and useful technological upgrades sit as if in unopened boxes, sets in.

As I'll explain more fully in Chapter 8, it is going to take a lot of goodwill and work from both sides to untangle this mess. But some simple steps can begin the process. It starts with understanding that data and IT are different sorts of assets that require different styles of management. This leads to more realistic expectations of information technologists, which should include providing basic storage, transport and processing capabilities, and automating well-defined processes to increase scale and decrease unit costs. With these foundations, more aggressive digital transformations, and simpler, more powerful, better data architectures to promote advanced data science can follow.

Eventually all change is top-down

I'm no expert on change management, but the sound bite, 'All change is bottom-up. All change is top-down' has stuck in my head for decades. It reflects the notion that new ideas come into a company through newer, younger, lower-level employees. Those ideas that pass muster make their way up the organization chart. First a department head, then a vice president, and eventually the CEO see their advantage and take them up. At the very least, more senior managers provide air cover so new ideas have a chance.

This is not happening in the data space. The best approaches to data quality, to small data, and to larger-scale data science have proven themselves, time and again. But senior management has shown itself unwilling or unable to take up the mantle of leadership to extend these techniques throughout their companies.

> In some ways I sympathize with senior leaders. Data, statistics and artificial intelligence are so ethereal. Unconsciously perhaps, they've dealt with bad data their entire careers and it hasn't held them back. Few of their colleagues or competitors seem interested. Worse, the data space is a large, untamed mess. There is simply no way the vast majority of senior leaders can know enough about data, where it fits, the issues and opportunities, and their roles.
>
> All this said, while my sample is not large enough to generalize, it appears that most truly want to help, but they don't know what to do. It leads me to conclude that an important task for the most senior data person, whatever their title, is 'training up the organization chart'.

The following vignette occurred in a discussion between myself and my client, an upper middle manager at a large multinational. He and others had got solid traction with data quality. Annual savings of hundreds of millions of dollars were in the works and it was clear that billion-dollar savings, across the company, were possible by simply copying the lessons learned. A large reorganization, the third in about five years, was also in the works. He was frustrated, but philosophical, that leadership had not understood this potential.

'Not to worry Tom,' he said. 'Once this reorganization takes place, we'll get another chance. We'll figure out where data fits.'

That didn't square with me and I responded, 'I think you have the sequence all wrong,' I said. 'I think the company needs to figure out what it wants to do about data first. Then reorganize. Until then, this cycle will continue.'

He thought about it for a moment, then had to agree. Unfortunately, he allowed, I was probably right. And the reorganizations have continued for more than a decade, data and people still afterthoughts.

To be clear, regular people and data teams can and should do more than they have. But unleashing the transformative power of data takes senior leadership. And indeed, leadership at the team and department levels has been an essential feature of all the success stories I know. Senior leaders, with real Cs in their titles, must step up to non-delegatable responsibilities: crafting the organization called for here; connecting data and business strategy; and building a culture that embraces data. More about this in Chapter 9.

New roles for data teams

Since their formation thousands of years ago, people, companies and governments have had to manage their data. For all but the last 50 years, almost all data was stored on paper. Offices had enormous file rooms and 'clerks', librarians and company historians did the work of labelling and storing the paper, helping people find what they needed, and retrieving it for them.

Large companies have also employed small numbers of specialists, often with advanced degrees in statistics, operations research, physics and related degrees, to innovate, to improve products and services, and to address particularly vexing problems.

Things changed as companies automated their back offices. Computers meant vastly more data stored on chips, not paper. In turn, a new class of data management professionals grew up to meet the growing and specialized needs for data architecture, integration, storage, warehousing and 'systems' to process it all. Most data professionals found their homes in management information systems, information technology and other groups.

Computers grew increasingly powerful and less expensive, pushing themselves out of the back office into every nook and cranny of modern life. Personal computers, mobile phones, and millions of other devices mean that managing much data falls to device owners, not professionals. Like it or not, regular people manage data, most often without training or support!

Further and relatively recently, companies have tried to do much more with their data in the mainstream portions of their businesses. This is no surprise; high-quality data and data science, artificial intelligence and data monetization offer considerable potential. Companies have hired chief data and/or analytics officers to lead their efforts, initiated data governance programmes, and/or created centres of excellence to pursue these goals. Most have fared poorly, for the reasons outlined in Chapter 2.

From my vantage point, it appears that companies have not thought enough about what they want their data teams to do, even without the new rigours imposed by regular people. Nor have they thought through where data teams fit into their existing organizations, preferring instead to simply 'bolt them on' to address what appear to be the most pressing needs. The legacy notion of subordinating data to the technologies used to move and manage it has led to many missteps. Finally, data is a mysterious asset, with properties unlike other assets such as people and capital. It is hard to manage something you don't really understand properly.

Companies need more from their data teams. They (data teams) must get much closer to regular people, help them understand and fulfil their new responsibilities; they must integrate advanced methods into business departments; and they must do a better job at enterprise issues such as common language. As noted earlier, an especially important task for the most senior data person is training 'up the organization chart' (Mai AlOwaish, Chief Data Officer at Gulf Bank, views this as her most important job). All of this will require fresh thinking. We'll tackle this subject in more detail in Chapter 10, orienting core data teams to these tasks. We'll also introduce embedded data managers, people 'embedded' in business teams and with close ties to professional data managers. Embeds understand the specific data challenges their departments face and lead efforts to address them.

Train to empower people and the company

While practically everyone can contribute to their team's and company's data efforts right away, the more people know, the more they can do. Over the long haul, the effort to help empower themselves, take on the responsibilities described here, and fight back the fear of entering the unknown are massive. Start with very basic ideas, especially people's roles as data creators and customers. Next, move to properly articulating business problems. But I am amazed by how few people can do so.

At Gulf Bank, Mai AlOwaish's team personally spends about 12 hours with ambassadors (Gulf Bank's name for the 'embedded data managers' of Figure 3.1) and one hour with everyone else. DBS Bank reports that it has trained 18,000 people in the basics of data management.[17] Eli Lilly and Travelers provide data and analytical literacy programmes for all their employees – and much of the content is tailored to the employee's level and business function.[18] They seem to be taking HG Wells to heart, viewing training as essential for all employees.

The Resource Centre at the end of this book aims to help: a toolkit describes eight tools to help people start the work called for here, and syllabi lay out the three courses regular people need now.

Create a sea change step-by-step

This discussion enables us to fill in the most important roles and responsibilities of Figure 3.1, presented as Figure 3.3. Taken together, they represent a sea change in the way data is managed and today – too much to address all at once!

So view Figure 3.3 as the long-term vision and build towards it a step at a time, based on business priorities. Most should start by engaging regular people in data quality – it provides the biggest short-term payback, builds human capabilities, and is on the critical path to everything else in the data space. After that, I anticipate companies will take many different paths.

FIGURE 3.3   Roles and responsibilities for each group in the proposed organization for data

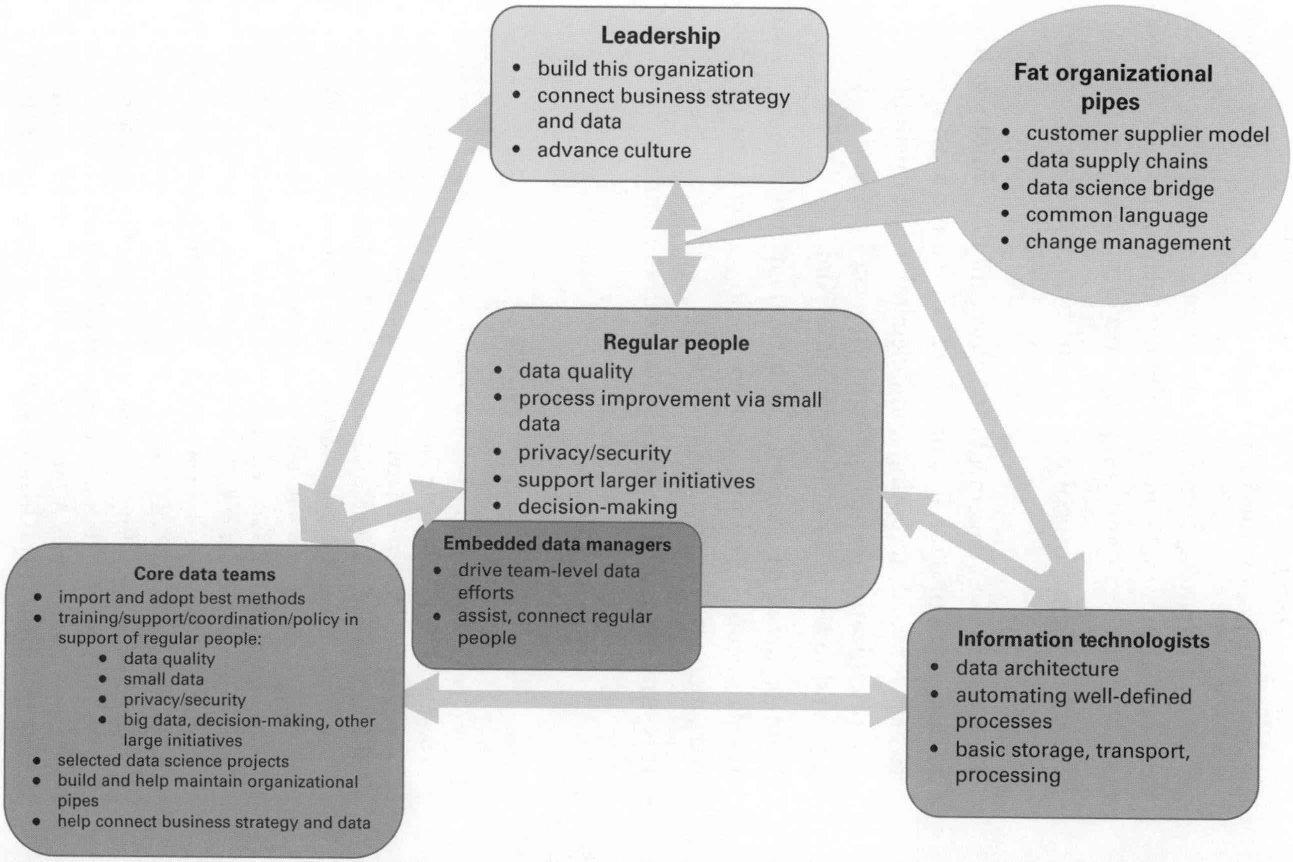

Fat organizational pipes
- customer supplier model
- data supply chains
- data science bridge
- common language
- change management

Leadership
- build this organization
- connect business strategy and data
- advance culture

Regular people
- data quality
- process improvement via small data
- privacy/security
- support larger initiatives
- decision-making

Embedded data managers
- drive team-level data efforts
- assist, connect regular people

Information technologists
- data architecture
- automating well-defined processes
- basic storage, transport, processing

Core data teams
- import and adopt best methods
- training/support/coordination/policy in support of regular people:
  - data quality
  - small data
  - privacy/security
  - big data, decision-making, other large initiatives
- selected data science projects
- build and help maintain organizational pipes
- help connect business strategy and data

Most important takeaways

The five most important points to put into practice soon include:

- First and foremost, companies must engage regular people in their data programmes. Doing so will help them improve their work life AND their team's and company's performance.
- Build fat organizational pipes to make it easier for people to work together.
- Separate the management of information technology from the management of data. It is time for a company's most senior leaders to get on board, accepting non-delegatable responsibilities to build the organization called for here, connect data and business strategy, and invest in a culture that values data.
- Data teams must reorient much of their programme to support regular people. Building and leveraging a network of embedded data managers accelerates this effort.
- It is time for senior leadership to get in the game.

Notes

1 Over the years, I've gradually introduced more and more of these ideas to my consulting clients. I first put the overall synthesis in the public domain in TC Redman, Build better management systems to put your data to work, *Harvard Business Review*, 30 June 2022, hbr.org/2022/06/build-better-management-systems-to-put-your-data-to-work (archived at https://perma.cc/G4BW-CXAS)

2 A recent study of corporate transformations supports this claim. See PA Argenti, J Berman, R Calsbeek and A Whitehouse. The secret behind successful corporate transformations, *Harvard Business Review*, 14 September 2021, hbr.org/2021/09/the-secret-behind-successful-corporate-transformations (archived at https://perma.cc/5R5Z-H9FL)

3 Quote from the presidential address in 1951 of mathematical statistician Samuel S Wilks (1906–64) to the American Statistical Association, found in *Journal of the American Statistical Association*, 46 (253), 1–18. Wilks was paraphrasing HG Wells (1866–1946) from his book *Mankind in the Making* (1903)

4 I assisted Ms Roopal in her research. She made this observation often during our conversations

5 J Moss. Beyond burned out, *Harvard Business Review*, 10 February 2021, hbr. org/2021/02/beyond-burned-out (archived at https://perma.cc/R9XE-R377)

6 TC Redman. Seizing opportunity in data quality, *MIT Sloan Management Review*, 27 November 2017

7 TC Redman. How to start thinking like a data scientist, *Harvard Business Review*, 13 November 2013, hbr.org/2013/11/how-to-start-thinking-like-a-data-scientist (archived at https://perma.cc/EY2W-5GRA)

8 TC Redman and RW Hoerl. Most analytics projects don't require much data, *Harvard Business Review*, 3 October 2019, hbr.org/2019/10/most-analytics-projects-dont-require-much-data (archived at https://perma.cc/UXN7-W22Q)

9 The manager actually said, 'We've drunk the Kool-Aid. And we're not going back.' 'Drunk the Kool-Aid' is slang in this company for 'we're fully bought in'. But some see it as a reminder of the mass killings at Jonesboro. So I've edited it

10 M Phelan (2020) *Freedom to be Happy: The business case for happiness*, self-published

11 (See also notes 12–16) TC Redman. To improve data quality, start at the source, *Harvard Business Review*, hbr.org/2020/02/to-improve-data-quality-start-at-the-source (archived at https://perma.cc/26K5-77WA)

12 TC Redman and RW Hoerl. Most analytics projects don't require much data, *Harvard Business Review*, 3 October 2019, hbr.org/2019/10/most-analytics-projects-dont-require-much-data (archived at https://perma.cc/7M9X-VLPC)

13 TC Redman and R Waitman. Do you care about privacy as much as your customers, *Harvard Business Review*, 28 January 2020, hbr.org/2020/01/do-you-care-about-privacy-as-much-as-your-customers-do (archived at https://perma.cc/5P45-8TSE)

14 TC Redman. Become more data-driven by breaking these bad habits, *Harvard Business Review* [blog] 12 August 2013, blogs.hbr.org/2013/08/becoming-data-driven-breaking/ (archived at https://perma.cc/A3CQ-9AA5)

15 TC Redman. Are you data-driven? Take a hard look in the mirror, *Harvard Business Review* [blog] 11 July 2013, blogs.hbr.org/2013/07/are-you-data-driven-take-a-har/ (archived at https://perma.cc/W9B5-NSTJ)

16 TC Redman. Your data initiatives can't just be for data scientists, *Harvard Business Review*, 22 March 2022, hbr.org/2022/03/your-data-initiatives-cant-just-be-for-data-scientists (archived at https://perma.cc/6GNE-YRGA)

17 DBS (2020) Annual Report, www.dbs.com/iwov-resources/images/investors/annual-report/dbs-annual-report-2020.pdf (archived at https://perma.cc/GP38-AAWH)

18 TH Davenport and N Mittal. How CEOs can lead a data-driven culture, *Harvard Business Review*, 23 March 2020, hbr.org/2020/03/how-ceos-can-lead-a-data-driven-culture (archived at https://perma.cc/2AV2-5B4L)

PART TWO

People

4

The data generation
and provocateurs

Empowering themselves

Meet the data generation

Most people have adopted a 'meh' attitude when it comes to data. While they need it to do their jobs, they are basically disengaged – dealing with mundane data issues and not looking for ways to use it to improve their teams' performance. Exacerbating this, many harbour legitimate fears that statistics, data science, artificial intelligence and/or digital transformation could change, even eliminate, their jobs. It is no wonder so many are beyond burnt out, 'quietly quitting', and/or resigning.[1]

This is unfortunate because today, data offers unprecedented opportunity to anyone willing to seek it out and seize it. Obviously, if you know more you can do more, but practically everyone, regardless of profession, age or level of training can do plenty. We'll explore the 'people' aspects of the opportunity in this chapter and dig into specific areas in the following two chapters.

CASE STUDY
Lesley

Lesley was a 41-year-old part-time marketing manager for a small company when the Covid-19 pandemic struck. She also had a husband and two rambunctious boys, aged 8 and 11. Like most working mums, she already had a full plate, even as she worked from home and was usually able to schedule her work around her kids' school schedules.

Covid impacted Lesley in many ways. First, her workload went up:

'I went from having four or five quiet hours at home every day to having two people needing continuous help – from getting online for class, to figuring out how to turn in assignments, to answering their questions about when they would see their friends. And I had to do a lot more real thinking at work – the things we did to reach possible clients just didn't seem to work. So this was really stressful.

'I noticed a change in myself first with their schools as they prepared to reopen after the summer. I know everyone was doing their best, but there never seemed to be any good answers. So I became more demanding. For example, I once told the head teacher, "Tell us what you really think will happen, not what you'd like to happen." A lot of parents told me they were glad I asked that.

'As Covid wore on, I found myself questioning the metrics I was using at work. Before, I had always tried to "meet my numbers". It was pretty clear I wasn't going to meet them during Covid, so I started to think longer term. Now I'm approaching my work more confidently – not just with more relevant numbers, but also in terms of what goes beyond the numbers.'

Most people have been remarkably tolerant of bad data and the time it wastes. That has begun to change recently as the day-in, day-out indignities associated with political misinformation, the pandemic, and the challenges in finding a new normal have fuelled a growing intolerance. Some people are concerned with big issues, such as 'How many people have really died from Covid?' and 'Can we trust election results?' But for most people, it has been the closer-to-home, more personal issues that have brought fresh urgency to high-quality data and analyses. Questions like:

- 'What percentage of people in my neighbourhood are fully vaccinated?'
- 'Your website says you have light blue paint. Where is it?'
- 'Can I believe this report about a philandering local official?' and
- 'Will the gifts I ordered arrive in time for the holidays?'

demand immediate, trusted answers.

In response, more and more people have quit tolerating bad answers and empowered themselves to find fuller, more complete, accurate and relevant data, and to use it to improve things in their personal, professional and civic lives. We call such people the Data Generation.

In effect, members of the data generation are seizing opportunities to improve data quality (Chapter 5) and put data to work (Chapter 6) on their own initiative in their personal, professional and civic lives.

CASE STUDY
Javier

For **Javier**, a 56-year-old sales manager for a consumer goods company, the impact of Covid came fast and furious:

'Like everyone else, we have systems that predict next quarters' sales down to the SKU level. I never liked them too much – they always gave me different numbers, but at least they were something. Then the pandemic hit and I didn't know what to do. The numbers really didn't change all that much, but all the tech people told me not to trust them – something about the training range being wrong.

'A lot of my competitors laid off half their staff. While I could see the fear in our senior management's eyes, we decided to wait – the company had done just fine in 2007 and 2008 during the last recession. For me, that was personal. My last company laid me off in early 2008 when things got rough. That's when I took this job.

'So I gathered my staff together to try to sort things out. Over Zoom we set up a couple of white boards, one labelled "what we think we know", the next "what we would like to know". Of course, it was easier to fill up the second board, but the more we thought about it, the more we realized we were pretty certain of a few key points. One was that our kids' candy products were pretty recession-proof. Even out-of-work parents would buy their kids a piece of our candy – it helps things seem more normal. This gave everyone confidence we were doing the right thing.

'I decided I was sick and tired of rationalizing three sets of numbers. So I dug into it and found out that we measured market share in three different ways. We're working to sort that out now!'

I find it highly significant that more regular people have empowered themselves with data at home than at work. I suspect that, while data problems at work are annoying, it is also easy to excuse them as 'just part of the job'. Personal issues came with a far bigger stake and greater urgency. Questions such as, 'When will my 8 and 11 year olds, whom I love deeply but are driving me crazy, be back in the class-room?' are simply more important than, 'Why don't the numbers from these two systems agree?' As the old saw advises, 'necessity is the mother of invention.'

Of course, there have always been members of the data generation. Many technical people, scientists and business analysts qualify. And every department has always had 'that guy', someone who could explain the numbers better than anyone else and was always happy to help. But the heart and soul of 'the data generation' are regular people who've empowered themselves. The case studies in this chapter tell the stories of five people (more accurately, 'personas', based on multiple individuals) who did just that.

You have the power

'Empowerment' is an interesting term. The basic idea is that those who have power should share it with those that don't. There are many good reasons to promote empowerment – diversity may prevent groupthink and lead to better outcomes, peace in the realm and simple fairness.

CASE STUDY
Daniel

Daniel graduated from college in 2014. He initially moved to the city but, due to the high cost of rent and finding suitable roommates, he moved back in with his parents in 2018. Growing up, his parents were very involved in local politics – his mum served on the school board and his dad on the town's planning commission. Daniel never thought too much about it.

When he moved back home, his parents' interest in politics had gone national. They watched the news every night and talked openly about their concerns for him and (when he had them) his children. Daniel also noticed a change in tone at the local Starbucks. Still, he remained disinterested.

That changed with the killing of George Floyd. Daniel had heard about racism of course. But his many Black, Spanish and Asian friends never said much about it. Still, Daniel's curiosity was piqued. So he began to talk to them privately about their experiences. While all had eye-opening stories to tell, the stories his Black friends told him frightened him. So he dug deeper, studying the *New York Times* '1619 Project' and other materials.[2]

As he learned more, Daniel began to engage his white friends. While some were indifferent, most came to see that they had benefited from being white. Following the grassroots politics example of his parents, Daniel assembled a collection of facts and stories and set a goal for himself of using them in discussion with one new person a week. 'Frankly,' Daniel observed, 'my parents' generation did lots of good things. But they didn't get anywhere with racism. Now it's up to people my age to work on this. I hope we can start with the facts.'

Finally, Daniel added, 'Now that my eyes are open, I see a lot of this at work. We make decisions basically because the boss says so. We don't even attempt to understand what is going on. I'm going to see if I can change that.'

These potential advantages aside, I've never seen it happen. Those who have power, may nod their heads and say the right things, but they don't give it up easily.[3] The bottom line is that people must empower themselves.

The good news is that almost all regular people have more power than they think they do. This is especially true in the data space. Bosses simply do not say, 'Whatever you do, don't improve quality' or 'I'm sorry, we're proud of our slow, ineffective and expensive processes. We don't want you sorting out ways to make them better.' Finally, as repeatedly emphasized, data programmes cannot succeed without the data generation. In a very real sense, companies need you more than you need them!

Building on this theme, Bob Pautke, a Cincinnati-based career advisor observes, 'Too many people have great ideas but are afraid to speak up. Data empowers them – it's not just your opinion when you have the facts to back you up.'[4]

Pick something

I find that almost everyone has plenty of ideas about how to improve things at work. It may involve working in a different way with a supplier, dealing with quality issues, talking to customers, or starting meetings on time. So pick something that interests you and dig in.

It is best to start small, with a first task you can complete in days, even a few hours. It is also best to enlist a colleague or two to join you. (The Toolkit provides step-by-step instructions for empowering yourself to communicate your needs (B), make a data quality measurement (C), complete a small data project (D), and start becoming a better decision-maker (E).)

Successfully completing one effort will build your confidence for the next, and the next, and pretty soon you'll be a fully-fledged member of the data generation! (To dispel your fears, these tools allow you to work 'below the radar'. So, if you fail no one will even know!)

CASE STUDY
Ahmed

Ahmed majored in Biology in college. He had planned to go to medical school but knew he didn't have a good enough GPA (grade point average). So he decided to seek an MS in Data Science instead. On completing his degree, he joined a regional bank that was just starting its data programme.

Ahmed's first project involved customer profitability. 'I spent long hours at my computer, working to wring the last bit of "unexplained variation" I could out of my models. I was proud of myself.' But no one on the business side knew how to use Ahmed's results. Everyone acknowledged he was very smart, but 'he doesn't know banking'.

'I vowed to spend more time learning how the business works,' Ahmed said. 'It was clear the bank wanted to grow, so I focussed on finding an under-served community to target. And I found a large, minority group that looked really promising.' But when he presented his results, senior managers again pushed back. How, they wanted to know, had Ahmed assured data quality? 'I didn't have a good answer and, when I looked at the data, I could see they had a point.'

'I don't know for certain,' Ahmed observed, 'But I felt I had been set up. So I decided to find a new job.' As he interviewed, Ahmed set a condition for his next employer – he insisted that someone close to the business be assigned to work with him on all his projects. Now just turning 30, Ahmed has had three solid successes at his new company – two small and one big enough to get his name mentioned in senior circles. He observes, 'I went to a top-flight school, but they didn't teach me about any of this soft stuff. I've learned my lesson.'

Use what you learn in your personal life at work – and vice versa

Interestingly, the methods you use to embrace data at work are exactly the methods you need to embrace data at home. So apply the lessons you learn at work to your personal life, and vice versa, to reinforce one another. To illustrate, the first step in any data quality project involves understanding who the customers are and what they need. This means active listening. While I learned these skills at work, they proved even more valuable as I tried to be a good parent to my teenagers. Conversely, I use skills gained in clearly explaining data science to my children to better communicate results to senior managers.

Think through 'What's in it for me?'

As you gain some experience with data, it's okay be a little selfish, asking yourself, 'what's in it for me?' Some tell me they experience a special satisfaction in conquering their fears of data and learning something new. Others use their successes with data to better position themselves for promotion. Conversely, some dispel their worry that failing to jump on board would limit their careers down the road. Many find a primal joy (the aforementioned joy youngsters feel in learning to ride a bike) in taking on a 'sacred cow', something that had always annoyed them at work. And so forth.

So think it through. Then craft the series of projects you work on to get what you want!

Provocateurs take things further[5]

Ms Wong

Ms Wong is a 25-year veteran elementary school teacher. She taught one of five third-grade classes at Public School 72 for six years. 'I love third graders,' Ms Wong observed.

'They know what school is all about and they are so curious. They say they don't like school, but you can see that they do. Third graders also hear everything. So it is no surprise that kids have all sorts of opinions on topics as diverse as "are boys smarter than girls?" to "whether the hot dogs were better than cheeseburgers in the cafeteria". We had lots of good discussions on such topics.

'Over the school year, we have a lot of parents come in to talk about their jobs. One mother's job was something I'd never heard of – data scientist. To illustrate what she did, she asked the kids questions about brushing their teeth. This evoked a lot of discussion. After a while she said, "All right, let's organize everyone's thoughts." She asked the kids to vote on a lot of things but two stand out in my mind: "Do you like to brush your teeth?" and "Do you use an electric toothbrush?"

'Then she made a little chart and asked the kids what they thought. They quickly saw that those who used electric toothbrushes liked brushing their teeth more. So she asked them why. Someone said, "It makes my mouth tickle" and everyone laughed. The next day two kids told me they'd asked their parents to get them electric toothbrushes.

'I really didn't like maths in college and I've probably emphasized teaching kids to read a bit too much. But this fascinated me. I asked that mother if I could copy what she did. Of course she said yes and helped me put a couple of lessons together. Now I use them three or four times a year. I've also learned to ask the kids, "Are you sure your data is accurate?" The kids really pick up on that!'

I cannot overemphasize the importance to individuals that they join the data generation. Doing so will make you happier and more productive. It is a big deal! And no complaints from me if you stop there.

But some people have gone much further, not just empowering themselves but leading work on major business problems for their teams, departments and companies. They may be the most important members of the data generation. I call them *provocateurs* because they show what is possible – *provoking* change, paving the way and inspiring others to join the data generation:

- The aforementioned Bob Pautke, then working at AT&T, wanted to improve his team's financial assurance processes. He didn't have a detailed enough understanding of those processes and needed to open them up to see how they worked. What he found led to AT&T completely rearranging financial assurance, saving his company hundreds of millions a year as a result.

- Jeff MacMillan, at Morgan Stanley, wanted to provide better risk management around the bank's clients. No one would openly admit there was a problem, but Jeff knew better. He thought he needed better data and sensed he would have to rethink the way his team approached their work to get it.

- Liz Kirscher had heard about the power of Six Sigma in manufacturing and wondered whether it would help Morningstar provide better data products.

- Stephanie Fetchen and Kim Russo at Tele-Tech Services wanted to position their company as the best in their niche.

- Karl Fleischmann, Brent Kedzierski, Tom Kunz, Randy Petit and Ken Self, in various parts of Shell, could see enormous waste and wanted to take costs out of the business.[6]

- Rob Goudey, at the EPA (Environment Protection Authority) in Victoria, Australia, knew the agency needed better data to build trust with citizens.[7]

- Don Carlson was trained as a mechanical engineer, and wanted to bring some of that discipline to data supply change management at Bank of America.[8]

- Maria Villar wanted to change her company's approach to managing data quality in ways that would outlive changes in management.[9]

- Zahir Balaporia wanted to apply what he learned from Total Quality Management on the factory floor to data and logistics.[10]

These people and plenty of others recognized a business problem. None knew exactly how to fix it, but they had the curiosity to dig deeper and find the facts. Then they put the facts to work, leading to enormous improvements in their teams' and companies' performance (making them members of the data generation). In providing a script for others to follow, they earned the title provocateurs!

It is tempting to cite Bob, Liz and all the others as rugged, courageous individualists, pushing back on corporate bureaucracy and persisting through thick and thin. But it is simply not true. All were great corporate citizens. They simply observed, 'This doesn't work very well' and pushed to make improvements. They needed better data to do so. That data signalled opportunity and they took it. Most started small, making one improvement at a time. All demonstrated success pretty quickly. They automated processes when they could and invested in people. They kept their bosses informed each step of the way. As they got traction, they secured funding to go further. All encountered, but none ran into concerted resistance. No magic involved.

I'm yet to meet anyone who doesn't have plenty of ideas about how to improve their team's work. I hope the experiences of these provocateurs empowers others to pursue their own ideas. After all, there is a little provocateur in all of us and it is time to let it out. Even if you're not up for that, join the data generation!

Implications for leaders, managers and data teams

If readers take just one idea from this book, I hope it is that data programmes need regular people, lots of them, to join the data generation. Companies also need provocateurs and they should count themselves lucky if two such people come forward. I've yet to sort out how companies can 'make' more of these special people – some just seem to come forward. If you're one of the lucky ones, nurture them as best you can, giving them plenty of latitude and keeping bureaucratic hurdles to a minimum.

The data generation can be the vanguard of the large numbers of regular people your data programmes need. Many can serve as embedded data managers, a role we'll discuss in greater detail in Chapter 10. This means leaders must get to know these people. As I've noted, many are far more proactive at home – the goal is to get them to bring that proactivity to work.

You should ask yourself why this is – is there something about your work environment that discourages people from trying out new ideas? I find that many managers harbour a preconception that 'people are part of the problem', and simply are not equipped to deal with data and/or are resistive to change. 'Why else would so few take initiative when it comes to data?' they reason. Of course, some employees are that way. But when I ask employees about it, many respond, 'No one ever asked.'

The quote betrays how preconceptions can get in the way. Managers must ditch them, adopting a new attitude in which they view people, or at least the data generation, as the key to the solution. This means having a little faith in people – giving them some space, and some responsibility. You may, for example, wish to assign people the tasks described in Tools C–F of the Toolkit.

An even better way is to do exactly what I'm asking everyone else to do – join the data generation. Follow the script laid out above: see opportunity for yourself, pick something to work on, complete one project using Tools C–G as appropriate, then complete another. After all, managers, including senior leaders, are regular people too!

The most forward-thinking leaders will come to see data as human empowerment, as a tremendous vehicle by which people can minimize the mundane parts of their jobs, take back a measure of control, learn new skills, have more fun at work and advance their careers. But even the least forward-thinking must put people at the centre of their organizations for data and ensure they get the training and support they need. We'll explore how embedded data managers and core data teams support these objectives in Chapter 10.

One organization that is doing all it can to get everyone involved is the United States Department of State. It is doing so via 'surges', data campaigns focussed on specific areas such as strategic competition with China, or workforce diversity, equity and inclusion. A 'campaign' brings everything in the data toolkit, from analytics, to quality, to basic data management, to training right to the workforce. Campaigns attract executive attention, leading to focus on the highest priority projects. While short, say six months, they also aim to leave the requisite skills in place when data teams move on to the next campaign.[11] Early results are positive, though it will take some time to confirm that benefits remain, especially after a change of leadership.

Most important takeaways

- The real heroes in the data space are provocateurs – the first in their teams and departments to tackle a significant business problem using data in new ways.
- Everyone should join the data generation, seeking more complete, accurate and relevant pictures of reality and putting what they learn to work, whether their companies ask them to do so or not. Almost all can make important contributions right now.
- Simultaneously, companies should seek to make the data generation as large and diverse as they can.
- To start, many managers need to change their attitudes, seeing potential in regular people.

Figure 4.1 displays a mix of regular people, members of the data generation, embedded data managers and provocateurs within a work team. Some (in time, hopefully, all) regular people join the data generation. Some will be enlisted to become embedded data managers and a few may become provocateurs.

FIGURE 4.1 The work team

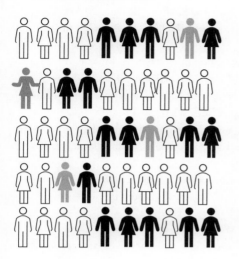
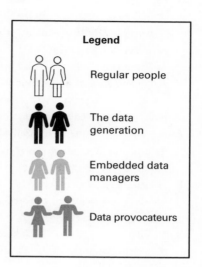

Notes

1 I'm well aware that some question the reality of 'The Great Resignation' and 'quiet quitting'. Personally, I suspect that the variation is enormous – some people are happy at work, some have always put in the bare minimum, some are always looking for better jobs. Still, it seems very likely to me that 'larger fractions of people are more burnt out', larger fractions fear that 'data, AI and digital transformation may dramatically alter, even eliminate, their jobs', and 'that more people than ever before are seeking more than a paycheck at work'. I worry about fear because it leads people and organizations to behave in unpredictable fashions. But opportunity awaits those who can get over their fears. See for example, TC Redman. Dispel your team's fear of data, *Harvard Business Review,* 16 July 2015, hbr.org/2015/07/dispel-your-teams-fear-of-data (archived at https://perma.cc/H93V-ZFAB)

2 The 1619 Project is a *New York Times Magazine* initiative that aims to reframe US history by placing the consequences of slavery and the contributions of Black Americans at its very centre, www.nytimes.com/interactive/2019/08/14/magazine/1619-america-slavery.html (archived at https://perma.cc/GEP4-67TV)

3 See, for example, R Greene and J Elffers (1998) *The 48 Laws of Power*, Viking

4 TC Redman. Three Steps to Joining the Data Generation, MyHRFuture, 21 April 2022, www.myhrfuture.com/blog/2022/4/20/three-steps-to-joining-the-data-generation (archived at https://perma.cc/9U7R-JC9Y)

5 Examples here taken from (see also notes 6–10): TC Redman. Data quality should be everyone's responsibility, *Harvard Business Review,* 20 May 2016, hbr.org/2016/05/data-quality-should-be-everyones-job (archived at https://perma.cc/MKF5-DMS6)

6 TC Redman. *Getting in front on data: Who does what,* Technics Publications, 2016; and a series of 'In Your Words' LinkedIn articles: T Kunz. 9 May 2017, www.linkedin.com/pulse/your-words-tales-real-life-data-provocateurs-tom-redman/ (archived at https://perma.cc/E7LZ-WMDM)

7 R Goudey. 13 June 2017, LinkedIn, www.linkedin.com/pulse/tales-real-life-data-provocateursin-words-rob-goudey-tom-redman/ (archived at https://perma.cc/WL73-28F8)

8 D Carlson. 2 November 2017, LinkedIn, www.linkedin.com/pulse/tales-real-life-data-provocateurs-your-words-don-carlson-tom-redman/ (archived at https://perma.cc/5CPP-F7TE)

9 M Villar. 8 August 2017, LinkedIn, www.linkedin.com/pulse/tales-real-life-data-provocateurs-words-maria-villar-tom-redman/ (archived at https://perma.cc/7XW5-YBGB)

10 Z Balaporia. 26 September 2017, LinkedIn, www.linkedin.com/pulse/tales-real-life-data-provocateurs-words-zahir-balaporia-tom-redman/ (archived at https://perma.cc/3YML-7XKY)

11 M Graviss and G Berntsen. Opinion: How do you make the State Department data-driven? One campaign at a time, Fedscoop, 28 September 2022, www.fedscoop.com/opinion-how-do-you-make-the-state-department-data-driven-one-campaign-at-a-time/ (archived at https://perma.cc/C7CC-DZYS)

5

All roads lead through quality

When trust leaves the room

George Schultz, US Secretary of State under Bill Clinton, on the importance of trust, famously remarked that:

> Trust is the coin of the realm. When trust was in the room, whatever room that was, the family room, the schoolroom, the government room or the military room – good things happened. When trust was not in the room, good things did not happen.[1]

The statement is eerily relevant today, in political domains all over the world. Left and right, Republicans and Democrats, globalists and nationalists are all further apart than ever. And the prospects for coming together seem dim.

Especially pertinent to our subject, nothing destroys trust like misinformation! It is corrosive, hardening positions, leading sides to demonize the other, and driving sides further apart, all in a seemingly endless vicious cycle. The best hope lies in starting with a reasonably complete, shared, set of 'facts' that all can agree are reasonably correct. As I previously noted, working towards such a situation may well represent THE political challenge of the 21st century.

GUILTY, TILL PROVEN INNOCENT

Many people trust sources of bad data and misinformation longer than they should. They are well aware of 'garbage in, garbage out', but persist in their belief that that it doesn't apply to them. They say things like 'it's in the computer so it must be right', 'our data is far better than most', and 'I know there are some problems with the data, but our models are just fine'. In effect, they adopt a 'good, till proven bad' ('innocent till proven guilty') attitude to data quality. And it can be hard for them to change their minds. It is a dangerous preconception, especially for data of unknown provenance.

I advise everyone to take the opposite perspective. Assume the data is bad. Give it a chance to prove itself innocent, but demand hard evidence! If the source cannot provide it, grow increasingly suspicious.

Finally, note that this advice applies not just in companies, but in your personal and civic life as well.[2,3]

While the details and the stakes differ, this linkage between bad data and poor trust inside many companies is eerily similar. I've already noted that only 3 per cent of data meets basic quality standards. Couple that with a *Harvard Business Review* research study that shows only about a sixth (16 per cent) of managers trust the data they use every day.[4] No wonder – if only 3 per cent meet basic quality standards, the data should not be trusted!

Evidently, trust has left the room when it comes to data!

Immediate consequences

Let's develop a more complete picture of the current state, starting with the estimate that only 3 per cent of companies' data meets basic standards. It is at the centre of Figure 5.1. Bad data adds enormous friction, or worse, to practically all work. Impacts include:[5]

- People must spend considerable time dealing with data quality issues. While there is considerable variation, the best estimate is that professionals spend about 50 per cent of their time dealing with mundane data issues, as they make corrections, resolve inconsistencies and seek confirmation to numbers that just don't look right.

- Correcting errors is hard work and some of them leak through. This adds further costs.

- Bad data leads to mistakes in day-in, day-out work, operations and decisions.

- The added work to deal with errors costs companies dearly. Again, there is considerable variation, but a good starting estimate is 20 per cent of revenue.

- The entire economy suffers. IBM puts the total cost of bad data at $3.1 trillion per year in the United States alone.

- Sometimes, far too often actually, people die:

  o Two Boeing 737 Max aircraft crashed because the angle of attack sensors provided faulty data. Some 346 lives were lost, the disasters cost Boeing at least $20 billion and the ripple throughout its supply chain cost many times as much.[6,7]

  o There is no telling how many people died needlessly due to bad Covid data. But a relatively localized, short-duration problem involving 43,000 false negative Covid tests in September 2021 is estimated to have led to between an additional 400 and 1,100 people's deaths.[8]

  o Unfortunately, this list could grow very long.

- Finally, bad data is especially harmful during times of crisis when, without data they can trust, leaders are essentially guessing:

  o Death and infection counts, positivity rates, and demographic factors are all essential for developing models of the progression of the disease, conducting 'what-if' analyses, and managing public policy – yet all are problematic.

  o Many people have lost faith in the US Centers for Disease Control and Prevention, viewed as a premier organization just a few years ago. Is it no wonder that the battles over plans for reopening have proven so brutal?[9,10,11,12,13,14,15]

  o Similar issues, while not as potentially lethal, have impacted all leaders trying to navigate the pandemic.[16]

These statistics should stagger any manager, even those who don't give a whit about data per se. Even ignoring the revenue potential that high-quality data can unlock, they fully justify an all-out attack on data quality.

FIGURE 5.1 Bad data and its impact: the headlines

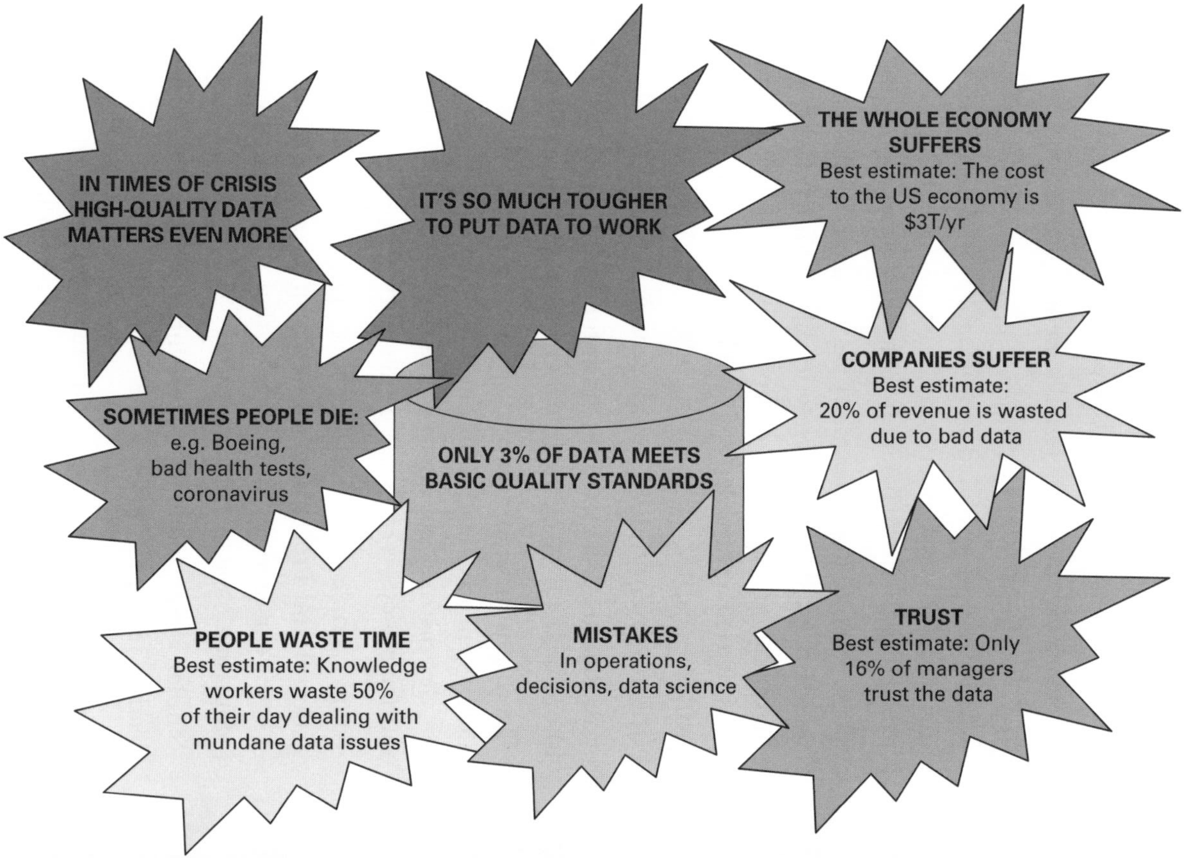

THE WHOLE ECONOMY SUFFERS
Best estimate: The cost to the US economy is $3T/yr

COMPANIES SUFFER
Best estimate: 20% of revenue is wasted due to bad data

TRUST
Best estimate: Only 16% of managers trust the data

IT'S SO MUCH TOUGHER TO PUT DATA TO WORK

ONLY 3% OF DATA MEETS BASIC QUALITY STANDARDS

MISTAKES
In operations, decisions, data science

IN TIMES OF CRISIS HIGH-QUALITY DATA MATTERS EVEN MORE

SOMETIMES PEOPLE DIE:
e.g. Boeing, bad health tests, coronavirus

PEOPLE WASTE TIME
Best estimate: Knowledge workers waste 50% of their day dealing with mundane data issues

Longer-term consequences

Next, looking to the future, bad data and the mistrust it engenders makes everything we hope to achieve with data more difficult. I include data science, monetization, digital transformation, data-driven decision-making, and the notion that data represents assets on this list. Start with data science, including machine learning and artificial intelligence, where bad data is an absolute plague (see the 'Data quality' box).[17] Since no analysis, insight or model is any better than the data on which it is based, data science projects must meet a high quality bar. But the issues are so common that the old expression 'garbage in, garbage out' simply will not go away. Indeed, it is being replaced by 'big garbage in, big garbage out'. At the risk of being repetitive, when the data is not to be trusted, you can't trust models or predictions stemming from even the most sophisticated artificial intelligence algorithm.[18,19]

As I noted in Chapter 2, many data scientists wish that someone else would deal with data quality issues for them. Good data scientists know better. And some go to extraordinary lengths to deal with data quality issues – up to 80 per cent of data scientists' time is spent this way.[20] But even if they do their jobs perfectly, getting over hurdles imposed by the latent mistrust is a tall order.

DATA QUALITY AND ADVANCED DATA SCIENCE

The data quality requirements for many uses of machine learning/artificial intelligence are extremely stringent, much higher than anything else. There are many reasons for this. First, the stakes are higher: while bad data may mean you send someone the wrong sweater or make a suboptimal decision, bad data and machine learning present the opportunity to screw up on a massive scale! Computers don't care whether the inputs are good or bad. After all, garbage in, garbage out!

A second reason the requirements are so stringent is that there are so many of them. The data used to train a model must have predictive power, be free from bias, carry massive amounts of metadata (e.g. definitions) with them, and have high levels of accuracy.

Third, there are both 'going back' and 'going forward' problems. 'Going back' issues involved the data used to train a model, while 'going forward' issues are those in data used by the model once it is switched on. While it may be possible to clean up bad data in training, it is a time-consuming, unpopular job. And it is not feasible to do so once the model is switched on. So these requirements must be met by the newly created data used as the model is put to work.

Finally, in more traditional data science, the analyses return parameters and coefficients, with real-world interpretations. If either doesn't make sense, you can question the model. But you may not get those with machine learning.

I cannot make this point strongly enough! Data science, especially AI and machine learning, are all the rage. But quality issues imperil all such efforts!

Continuing, it is hard to make a business selling data when it can't be trusted. Who would buy it?

Bad data enfeebles digital transformation, the whole idea of which is to reimagine and automate business processes. But these processes depend on data and automating them just adds chaos.

Perhaps the most transformative uses of data involve data-driven decision-making, data-driven cultures, and treating data as assets. But again, bad data stymies such efforts. Promoting the notion that people should use data they don't trust to make decisions is a non-starter. Similarly, if you want to treat data as assets, it would be good to put them on the balance sheet as such.[21] But bad data can only be judged liabilities.

A course correction is desperately needed

Simply improving business performance today and building a long-term future in data depend on quality. Even if they lack the cold, hard facts to prove it, and no matter how much they wish it wasn't true, people know, deep in their hearts that data can't be trusted. They will not, and should not, fully embrace it. One can only conclude that broad acceptance of everything in the data space depends on broad acceptance that the data can be trusted. There is much to do!

The good news is that companies can make the needed improvements by changing their approach from reactively dealing with bad data to creating it correctly, the first time. This means getting regular people to step into roles as data creators and data customers and proactively attacking the root causes of error. Quality improves quickly and since people have helped make the improvements, trust follows, albeit more slowly.

Getting everyone onboard may seem like an impossible mission. But companies don't think twice about asking people to follow HR, finance or safety policies, even though they may personally feel no benefit. Exacerbating this, some complain that data quality is the least sexy of all data work.[22] But done well, most enjoy the work. And they certainly enjoy spending less time on mundane issues and more on their real work.

The remainder of this chapter explores what data quality involves more deeply, how people and companies came to address it improperly, and what proactively attacking data quality entails.

Data quality is more complex than you might expect

Consider the following vignette. Late one afternoon, as you're commuting home from work, you receive a call from the principal at your teenager's school. They have been suspended for fighting. Three days and a black mark on their permanent record.

When you get home you seek your child out, asking, 'How was your day?'

'Well,' they say as they show you an exam, 'I got a B+ on my Spanish test.'

If you were annoyed at the kid before, you are furious now! The child has certainly told the truth, providing a fact that would certainly interest you on most days. But not today. That truth is not enough. Their answer has to be relevant to the real question at hand, even though you did not explicitly ask, 'Did you get suspended from school today?'

To be of high quality, data must be both right (that is correct) and the right data for the task or question at hand. There is a lot going on here. The data being right is simplest. Essentially it means that the data must be correct enough to complete the operation, make the decision or properly feed a model. Thus, 'about US $70 billion' might be perfectly appropriate to a casual question, 'What was Google's revenue in 2020?' But it certainly wouldn't do for an SEC filing.

The 'right data' also depends on who is using the data and what they are using it for. In some situations, such as day-in, day-out operations, sorting out the right data is usually straightforward. If you sell sweaters on your website and deliver them by mail, you need to know who ordered what sweater (size, style, colour, etc), where they would like it delivered, and some billing details. In increasingly complex decision-making settings, sorting out the right data is increasingly difficult. Determining where to locate a warehouse may involve dozens of factors. Here 'right' requires a complete, diverse collection of data.

> Thus, *high-quality data* means the right data to complete the operation, to make the decision, etc, AND that the data is right, and correct enough for that purpose. We refer to this as the 'right, right data'. It is a stiffer standard than most expect.[23]

There are some situations where other features are required. A barcode scanner needs the data presented in a different format than other computers and human beings do – the right, right data presented in the right way. In other situations, data models, data definitions or lineage may be important. Finally, it bears repeating that the quality standards for advanced data science are extremely high.

Why data goes bad

Consider this vignette.

> Stephanie, an up-and-comer at Upscale Sweater (recall Ann, from Chapter 1 – Stephanie is her boss) is making final preparations for her first meeting with the Board. Her assistant walks into her office and says, 'Boss, something looks really wrong with the numbers from the Widget department.'
>
> 'Oh my gosh!' she exclaims. 'I can't present bad numbers to the Board. You have to fix them.'
>
> And off he goes. An hour later he reports back – he found the problem, changed the offending numbers in her slides and emailed her the final presentation.
>
> The Board meeting the next morning couldn't have gone better. They liked her and she liked them. In fact, the linchpin of the discussion revolved around those numbers her assistant adjusted.
>
> Of course, she is on cloud nine! She walks back to her office and is so happy she gives her assistant an on-the-spot award and the rest of the day off. As he's leaving she says, 'You know, you ought to check the Widget department's numbers every month.'

It's easy to feel good for Stephanie. She had a great day.

But not so fast! This story is wrong, on so many levels. Note what I didn't mention. Stephanie did not verify her assistant's changes. For all we know, the numbers he changed were correct all along. Or he could have made slightly bad numbers worse.

Stephanie didn't even have the courtesy to let the Widget department know there was a problem. In the absence of any feedback, the Widget department has no chance to sort out the root cause of the error or even make corrections. Worse, she left others in the company to be victimized by the bad data. Stephanie's actions, or rather lack thereof, sowed the seeds for further mistrust of the Widget department!

Finally, in asking her to check the numbers each month, she took responsibility for Widget numbers going forward, even though she doesn't know the first thing about them. Perhaps she had a good reason to mistrust the Widget department – more likely she simply lacked the creativity to see that there was a better approach.

The Stephanie vignette plays out in every department in every company every day. Recall the daisy chain of data – the Sales group receives data from Marketing, in turn passing new data onto Operations, and so forth. Even though there are lots of errors, salespeople have quotas. On any given day, it is simply easier to correct the data and get on with their work. A different motivation than presenting good numbers to the Board, but just as immediate and real. Sales and Operations people do their best, today, the next, and the day after that, never thinking to reach back to the source of the problem.

I call this cycle 'the hidden data factory' and it is presented in Figure 5.2, with one additional feature – correcting errors in real time.[24] Some errors leak through to the next steps, causing further damage and sowing further mistrust.

The hidden data factory is very expensive. The Rule of Ten (which is not a 'rule' but rather a 'rule of thumb') states that if it costs 1 dollar (pound, dinar, euro, etc) to complete a unit of work when the data is perfect, then it costs 10 when the data is not.[25] In its various guises, the hidden data factory does much to explain the 50 per cent of people's time wasted, the 20 per cent of revenue, and the $3.1 trillion/ year costs in the United States cited above.

FIGURE 5.2 The hidden data factory

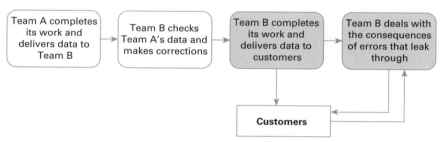

NOTE Steps in the grey boxes constitute work to accommodate data errors

A rush to automate

Most companies tacitly accept the hidden data factory. It has become so embedded in their business practices they can't imagine a different approach. But they can imagine two steps:

1 Automating the hidden data factory. And there is a cottage industry of companies eager to provide software to help. Indeed, sooner or later, most companies and departments seek to automate their hidden data factories.

2 Turning the hidden data factory over to a team of clean-up professionals, perhaps located within a core data team or the Tech department.

Sooner or later, most companies take these steps. It feels satisfying to feel you've done everything you possibly can! Imagine the relief felt by Stephanie's assistant when he no longer had to check Widget department numbers every month.

Unfortunately, these steps don't work.

One problem is that they move responsibility for quality even further from the Widget department. A second is that while much software is pretty good at finding errors, correcting them is much harder, usually requiring people. Worst of all, the hidden data factory never goes away!

As the quantity and variety of data you need grows, so too does the size of the hidden data factory. Just imagine that Stephanie had installed a software programme that cleaned all Widget data perfectly, but had not addressed the problem of poor quality at the source. Thus, as she acquires new Widget data, her assistant will once again waste time dealing with errors.

The hidden data factory as the means to ensure data quality is long past its sell-by date, even as people are drawn to it like moths to a flame.

A better way

The way to resolve data quality issues such as those between Stephanie and the Widget department, or between Sales and Marketing, is stunningly simple: work together to find and eliminate the root causes of the problems, that is, create the data people need correctly, the first time.

To see how this plays out in practice, consider what happened at one health clinic. Staff often had difficulties contacting patients post-visit when they needed to schedule more tests, change medications, and so forth. No one knew how frequently this occurred or exactly how much time was wasted, but it could impact patients' health and it was frustrating for the staff.

So employees in the clinic made a simple measurement (technically a FAM, described in Chapter 2): they checked and found that the contact number was wrong 46 per cent of the time. They reviewed their procedures and found that no one was responsible for obtaining that data. They made a simple change: when patients checked in, the front-desk person asked them to verify their phone numbers. It was the first thing they requested upon arrival: 'It is nice to see you again, Ms Jones. Can I confirm your cell phone number?' This clinic re-measured a couple of weeks later – errors in cell phone numbers were virtually eliminated.

The process the health clinic used – sort out the needed data, measure its quality, identify areas where quality must be improved, and identify and eliminate root cause(s) – is broadly applicable, remarkably flexible, easy to teach and simple to use.

THERE ARE A FEW REALLY COMPLEX DATA QUALITY ISSUES

While I don't have hard statistics, I find that most, maybe 80 per cent, of data quality issues can be resolved by following the method used by the health clinic. This may require reaching across department and company boundaries and is sometimes political. But most issues can be resolved because both creators and customers share high-quality data as a common goal.

Quality issues involving the 'right data' and those requiring groups to share a common language can be more difficult. Finally, a few may prove unsolvable, at least early on.

So smart people and companies start with the simpler issues!

Digging deeper, you see that the health clinic also features the two most important roles in data quality: the data customer and the data creator. The customer is the person using the data, the creator is the person who creates the needed data. Note that machines, devices and algorithms also use and create data. So the customer and creator may also be the person responsible for such machines, devices and algorithms.[26]

It is imperative that regular people, including managers such as Stephanie and senior leaders, step into these roles. They must recognize themselves as customers, clarify their needs and communicate those needs to creators. Failing to do so is the most important way Stephanie went wrong.

Regular people must also recognize themselves as creators, and make improvements to their processes, so they provide data in accordance with their customers' needs. In the health clinic, post-visit staff did not recognize themselves as customers and desk personnel did not recognize themselves as creators. Once they did, completing the improvement project was straightforward.

The business case for data quality

Quality improves quickly when teams and companies adopt this approach, take on these roles and follow these steps. People in companies large and small, in industries as diverse as financial services, oil and gas, retail and telecom, have used them to make order-of-magnitude improvements in billing, customer, people, production, and other types of data and, as a direct result, improved their team's performance.[27] Indeed, I don't know of any other way.

My best estimate is that you can permanently shrink the hidden data factory by three-quarters, or 15 per cent of revenue! And trust grows as improvements are made. A one-time clean-up of legacy data may be required. But one-time is a big improvement over every day.

These savings are important because other aspects of the data programme (e.g. big data, people) require investment. All by itself a well-run data quality programme can provide the savings needed to fund those investments for those investments.[28]

Many find this work transformational

At the risk of repeating myself, almost everyone prefers eliminating root causes to dealing with errors every day. And many find the effort transformational. I opened the Introduction to this book with a woman saying 'this is the first time I had any control' and quoted a manager saying 'We aren't going back'. Sabeeka AlRashed at Gulf Bank noted that the enthusiasm grows the more people get involved. 'As more people become engaged in this effort, you can see the whole bank changing.'

Further, quality spells opportunity for regular people. Plenty of Stephanies and other regular people have done just that, seeing for themselves the power of this approach, these roles, and the opportunity to make a difference. There is no need to wait for the company-wide programme. Practically anyone can become a better data customer and data creator. As mentioned in Chapter 4, data quality is a great way to empower yourself (and join the data generation in the process!). And if you're unsure how to get started, see Tools B (customer needs analysis) and C (Friday Afternoon Measurement) in the Toolkit.

Leadership, core data teams and embedded data managers required

While practically any regular person can take on data quality, relatively few do so unbidden. So it is up to senior leadership, core data teams and embedded data managers to play the roles sketched for them in Chapter 3. In particular, senior leadership must demand wholesale improvements, including holding departments and ultimately people accountable. Core data teams must build support for the effort, coordinate the work, specify the methods to be used, establish the metrics used to track progress, set targets for improvement; provide considerable training and handholding; and drive an aggressive change management plan. Embedded data managers sit between core teams and regular people, leading the effort within their teams.

Implications

It is vitally important that companies attack data quality properly. You're not going anywhere in the data space without high-quality data and you can earn some real savings, build trust and empower people along the way. I want readers to see the transition from today's efforts to find and fix errors to creating data correctly the first time, through a variety of perspectives (see Table 5.1).

None of the transitions suggested in Table 5.1 are intellectually challenging, but they do represent a paradigm shift, and those are always hard. It means holding departments and ultimately people accountable; considerable training and handholding; some well-placed metrics; building leadership support; and an aggressive change management plan. Today, the logical place to lead this work is from

TABLE 5.1 Most important features of the two main approaches to data quality

Perspective	From: Finding and fixing errors	To: Creating data correctly the first time
Management accountability	Those using data are (implicitly) responsible for its quality	At a granular level, accountability is (explicitly) shared between data customers and creators
		At a higher level, teams and departments, not some core group, are responsible for the quality of data they touch
Approach	React to errors, most often in the course of day-in, day-out work	Create data correctly the first time Attack: proactively prevent errors
Most important 'pros'	The way people think now	Quality higher, costs lower
Most important 'cons'	Expensive/doesn't work well	Requires a change in thinking and some investment
Tools used	Experience, business rules, tools that automate the work	Requirements, feedback, measurements, root cause analysis
Job satisfaction	Low. Finding errors is time-consuming, frustrating work that detracts from the main job	Most people enjoy the work and many find it transformational

core data quality teams. As discussed in Chapter 3, many of them must shift their own paradigms as well.

Most important takeaways

- Poor quality data is a brutal killer, sometimes quite literally. It adds enormous cost and erodes trust. For advanced data science, poor data is especially crippling.
- Improving quality dramatically should be the first priority for (almost) all companies.
- For regular people, improving data quality is the single best way to do something important and make a mark for themselves in the data space.
- Sexy or not, companies must change their approach to data quality, proactively attacking root causes.
- This means getting everyone involved as data customers and creators.
- Over time, companies should raise their expectations of regular people with respect to data quality.
- Smart companies will go further, seeing quality as human empowerment, providing needed training, and turning people loose.

Notes

1 GP Schultz. The 10 most important things I learned about trust over my 100 years, *The Washington Post*, 11 December 2020, www.washingtonpost.com/opinions/2020/12/11/10-most-important-things-ive-learned-about-trust-over-my-100-years/ (archived at https://perma.cc/5EZK-5XTW)

2 The interrelationships between trust and misinformation are many and fascinating. See 'This article is full of lies', *The Economist*, 2 November 2019, 52–54, for a discussion

3 For one way to evaluate whether data can be trusted, see TC Redman. Can your data be trusted, *Harvard Business Review*, 29 October 2015, hbr.org/2015/10/can-your-data-be-trusted (archived at https://perma.cc/B7EL-BA3W)

4   Qlik. Data and organizational issues reduce confidence, *Harvard Business Review*, 2013, https://issuu.com/bsgmanager/docs/wp-hbr-pulse-survey-en (archived at https://perma.cc/K2X3-S8RT)

5   In the article 'Seizing opportunity in data quality', I synthesized many sources for the statistics cited in this paragraph. See *MIT Sloan Management Review*, 27 November 2017, sloanreview.mit.edu/article/seizing-opportunity-in-data-quality/ (archived at https://perma.cc/CEF7-6ZVM)

6   There are thousands of references to these tragedies. For example (see also note 7): C Devine and D Griffin. Boeing Relied on a single sensor for 737 Max that had been flagged 216 times to FAA, CNN, 30 April 30 2019, www.cnn.com/2019/04/30/politics/boeing-sensor-737-max-faa/index.html (archived at https://perma.cc/PT55-FRKA)

7   C Isidore. Boeing's 737 Max debacle could be the most expensive corporate blunder ever, CNN, 17 November 2020, www.cnn.com/2020/11/17/business/boeing-737-max-grounding-cost/index.html (archived at https://perma.cc/8ZN2-C79Z)

8   *The Economist*. Botched covid-19 test results in Britain led to thousands of extra cases, 20 November 2021, www.economist.com/graphic-detail/2021/11/20/botched-covid-19-test-results-in-britain-led-to-thousands-of-extra-cases (archived at https://perma.cc/9E4F-JBV3)

9   Hundreds of articles have been, and will be, written on this topic. I've relied on the following sources (see also notes 10–15) to reach the conclusions cited here. G Davenport and TC Redman. To fight pandemics, we need better data, *Sloan Management Review*, 25 August 2020, sloanreview.mit.edu/article/to-fight-pandemics-we-need-better-data/ (archived at https://perma.cc/WDS9-T647)

10   Schechtman and Simon. Silent data mismatches are compromising key Covid-19 indicators, The Atlantic, 9 February 2021, covidtracking.com/analysis-updates/silent-data-mismatches-are-compromising-key-covid-19-indicators (archived at https://perma.cc/74DJ-PC22)

11   UL McFarling. The Uncounted: People who are homeless are invisible victims of Covid-19, STATNews, 11 March 2021, www.statnews.com/2021/03/11/the-uncounted-people-who-are-homeless-are-invisible-victims-of-covid-19/ (archived at https://perma.cc/HM8C-5Z4U)

12   Z Tufekci. The CDC needs to stop confusing the public, *New York Times*, 8 August 2021, www.nytimes.com/2021/08/04/opinion/cdc-covid-guidelines.html (archived at https://perma.cc/9NPT-8LMF)

13   Y Abutaleb and LH Sun. How CDC data problems put the US behind on the delta variant, *The Washington Post*, 19 August 2021, www.washingtonpost.com/health/2021/08/18/cdc-data-delay-delta-variant/ (archived at https://perma.cc/8XMV-BJFQ)

14 B Blauer and J Nuzzo. Covid-19 data is a mess. We need a way to make sense of it, *New York Times*, 23 November 2020, www.nytimes.com/2020/11/23/opinion/coronavirus-testing.html (archived at https://perma.cc/XJ7A-H6F8)

15 J Achenbach and Y Abutaleb. Messy, incomplete US data hobbles pandemic response, *The Washington Post*, 30 September 2021, www.washingtonpost.com/health/2021/09/30/inadequate-us-data-pandemic-response/ (archived at https://perma.cc/NH8X-R392)

16 TC Redman. Fighting misinformation, and building trust, in a crisis, tomredman.medium.com/fighting-misinformation-and-building-trust-in-a-crisis-982179f0dafc (archived at https://perma.cc/V9JS-78QP)

17 TC Redman. If your data is bad, your machine learning tools are useless, *Harvard Business Review*, 2 April 2018. (In retrospect, a better title would have been, 'If your data is bad, your machine learning tools are dangerous'.) hbr.org/2018/04/if-your-data-is-bad-your-machine-learning-tools-are-useless (archived at https://perma.cc/GZ8U-GAT3)

18 For an excellent discussion see: A Thurai and J McKendrick. Overcoming the C-suite's distrust of AI, *Harvard Business Review*, 23 March 2022, hbr.org/2022/03/overcoming-the-c-suites-distrust-of-ai (archived at https://perma.cc/QE4Y-M2N3)

19 I am pleased that Andrew Ng, one of the leading lights in AI, is recognizing the importance of quality data. See: G Press. Andrew Ng launches a campaign for data-centric AI, 16 June 2021, Forbes.com, www.forbes.com/sites/gilpress/2021/06/16/andrew-ng-launches-a-campaign-for-data-centric-ai/?sh=7b4c41c74f57 (archived at https://perma.cc/P5K3-ZSR3)

20 A Google search will reveal many sources for statistics on how much time data scientists spend on mundane data issues. To some degree, the answer depends on what exactly counts. Suffice it to say the fraction of their time is large. See in particular: CrowdFlower. 2016 Data Science Report, visit.figure-eight.com/rs/416-ZBE-142/images/CrowdFlower_DataScienceReport_2016.pdf (archived at https://perma.cc/6QWR-QJVL)

21 DB Laney (2018) *Infonomics: How to Monetize, Manage and Measure Information as an Asset for Competitive Advantage*, Bibliomotion Inc

22 TC Redman. If you don't find data quality sexy, you're not doing it right, *Melissa Magazine*, Summer 2018, 6–7, www.melissa.com/resources/magazines/essentials-for-data-driven-success/#p=6 (archived at https://perma.cc/A5BT-ZWNV)

23 TC Redman. Demand the (right) right data, *Harvard Business Review* [blog], 8 March 2012, blogs.hbr.org/cs/2012/03/demand_the_right_right_data.html (archived at https://perma.cc/3NY8-J2UF)

24 T Redman. Bad data costs the US $3.1t/year, *Harvard Business Review*, 22 September 2016, hbr.org/2016/09/bad-data-costs-the-u-s-3-trillion-per-year (archived at https://perma.cc/5TBG-46SN); T Redman (2016) *Getting in Front on Data: Who does what*, Technics Publications

25 I first introduced the Rule of Ten Factory in: TC Redman (2008) *Data Driven: Profiting from your most important business asset*, Harvard Business School Press. Some have expanded it to make a 1–10–100 rule, in recognition of the fact that error correction is hard work, so some errors will leak through to customers. The rule recognizes it can cost 100 times more to deal with these errors than had the data been error-free

26 TC Redman. To improve data quality, start at the source, *Harvard Business Review*, 10 February 2010, hbr.org/2020/02/to-improve-data-quality-start-at-the-source (archived at https://perma.cc/C4XK-5UP6)

27 TC Redman. Seizing opportunity in data quality, *MIT Sloan Management Review*, 27 November 2017, sloanreview.mit.edu/article/seizing-opportunity-in-data-quality/ (archived at https://perma.cc/F68S-GWPS)

28 TC Redman and TH Davenport. Getting serious about data and data science, *MIT Sloan Management Review*, 28 September 2020, sloanreview.mit.edu/article/getting-serious-about-data-and-data-science/ (archived at https://perma.cc/93JQ-6FGD)

6

Putting data to work

All by itself, improving data makes things better. Processes work better, decision-makers can make better decisions, it is easier to align people when they agree on the facts, and people feel empowered. It is important stuff. And there are many ways for individuals to put high-quality data to work, improving processes, products and services; creating new value, and new customers; and, in some cases, erecting barriers that are hard for competitors to match (see the 'Putting data to work' box).

The potential is enormous. I've already pointed out how disruptive Uber has been, simply by capturing and combining two pieces of data: 'I'm looking for a ride' and 'I'm looking for a fare' (Chapter 2). Uber explains why so many people are so excited about putting data to work. It also illustrates, once again, why high-quality data is so important and why data scientists are in such high demand.

'PUTTING DATA TO WORK' VERSUS 'MONETIZING DATA'

The phrase to 'monetize data' has gained a measure of acceptance. It certainly does fit when the goal is to 'sell' the data, either on its own or as part of some other product/service. But the goal isn't always strictly monetary. 'Improving patient outcomes' in a healthcare facility, 'improving safety' in a factory, and 'promoting equality' may all result from better use of data, even if they don't improve the bottom line. So I prefer the phrase 'putting data to work'.

At the same time, Uber isn't going anywhere if regular people don't sign up as drivers and as riders–users of the service!

One overarching theme in this chapter is that companies must do a far better job of embracing regular people in their data science efforts. I'll show why by dissecting the data science process, showing how regular people are essential each step of the way. The second theme is opportunity for both companies and regular people; specifically, both companies and regular people should redouble their efforts to put data to work. I'll also discuss several specific missed opportunities, which all signal opportunity for both regular people and companies.

Regular people and the data science process

First consider data science, including Big Data, advanced analytics, machine learning and artificial intelligence. To clarify why data science projects require regular people, let's unpack the 'data science process', as presented in Figure 6.1.[1] In reviewing each step, note the critical role played by regular people.

FIGURE 6.1 The data science process

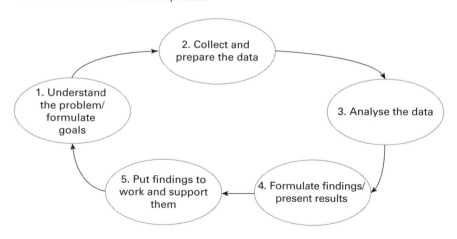

1 *Understand the problem/formulate goals*: First, the data scientist must develop a deep understanding of the business problem and the larger context in which it resides. Without doing so, data science is just a fishing expedition. It is simply not reasonable to expect data scientists to understand the overall business and the specific problems they can attack unless regular people explain their views of business direction, their work processes, the problems they experience, their views of needed improvements, and so forth. In failing to do these things, too many companies set their data scientists up to fail, figuratively sticking them in a room, giving them access to oceans of data, and saying, 'you figure it out'.[2]

NOTE: To be fair, data scientists often contribute to this problem. They may be too naïve to know how important it is to understand, too junior to know how to engage, too meek to admit they don't fully understand, or too confident in their abilities to find 'the answer' that will stun everyone. They must step up as well.

2 *Collect (and prepare) the data*: In some cases, data scientists design and run experiments to gather needed data. More often, they seek to leverage data the company already has. Data scientists have to develop a deep understanding of this data – what it covers (and what it doesn't), how it is defined and was collected, what units are used or how it has been measured, strengths and weaknesses, and so forth. None of this is possible without regular people.

3 *Analyse the data*: Ah, you might think – here is some work a data scientist can actually do on their own. Not so fast. First, as noted in the previous chapter, the data is usually of poor quality and data scientists need help putting it into reasonable shape. Further, data analysis/science is very much an iterative process – back and forth between the data and the world from which it comes. The data scientist sees something interesting in the data, sorts out if it squares with their understanding of reality, asks new questions, looks at the data in new ways, develops a theory about what it means, tests it, and so on. Obviously data scientists are equipped to look at the data in lots of ways, but aligning the insights from the data with the ways reality works requires regular people.

4 *Formulate findings/present results:* As the analyses are completed, data scientists present their results and their implications to decision-makers, the regular people we've talked about throughout. Findings may come in many forms: from simple summaries of the most important results, to recommended courses of action, to new models for use within a business process. Data scientists must get to know their audiences and present findings in appropriate, powerful ways. Regular people can help on both accounts. At this point, decision-makers decide whether, and if so, how, to move these findings forward. No support and the process terminates, with no value to the business.

5 *Put findings to work and support them:* Taking findings forward depends largely on regular people. For example, while findings may be built into a product, much like any other computerized system or application, success still depends on regular people using that application. No use, no value to the business! Even more importantly, regular people must deal with data quality issues going forward. (To be clear, data scientists have to do far more than most are doing in this step – there are people to train, models to keep current, and business benefits to summarize.)

Every step depends on regular people! This point is so important that it bears repeating in Table 6.1.[3]

TABLE 6.1 Roles for regular people in data science projects

Step	Roles for regular people	Consequences if the role is not served
1. Understand problem/ formulate goals	Clarify overall business direction and the problem to be solved	Data science becomes a fishing expedition
2. Collect data	Explain how the data is defined and created, any nuances, strengths and weaknesses	Risk that data scientist doesn't understand the data
3. Analyse data	Participate in discussion of interim results, initial theories, etc	Risk that results are less relevant and/or feasible
4. Present findings	Make decisions regarding how findings will be taken forward	Project stops, with no value to the business
5. Put findings to work and support them	Help embed findings in work processes and use them	Projects stops, with no value to the business

Ideally, data scientists and regular people team up, working side-by-side, beginning-to-end. And of course, many data science projects do just that. For example, Angelique Augereau, then Treasury CDO at JP Morgan, emphasized designing easy-to-use solutions from the very beginning.[4] At Disney, data efforts build on Disney's long-time emphasis on guest experience to help drive decisions throughout the company.[5] Research at McKinsey confirms the importance of building the trust it takes for people to embrace AI.[6] Finally, Tom Davenport has called out the shift to 'collaborative analytics'.[7]

Some companies are taking this even further. As Huzaifa Syed of Home Depot explained:

> We're using pods, for example, a marketing team is not just a team that focussed on audience strategy any more but also data science, measurement, paid media, creative, adops/reporting, owned media, earned media, onsite experience. And guess what – all the work that happens in these teams, every decision made, is based on data; for example, did one particular creative idea work better than the other? Or do we have the right people in our audiences? How effective was the onsite versus offsite experience for our customers? Data science is driving the data adoption in the pod structures and it's amazing to see how numbers can make wonders.[8]

Like everything in data, data science is a team sport. In part, this means holding teammates accountable. So regular people must demand beginning-to-end commitment from their data scientists as well.

Now let's consider several areas where both regular people and companies have missed opportunities, so far anyway.

The big pleasures of small data

Unless the quantities of data are very large or the analytic tools needed are especially complex, no step of the data science process requires a data scientist. Quite the contrary. If the quantity of the needed data is relatively small and can be analysed using basic methods, small teams of regular people (with just a bit of assistance) can navigate the process just fine. Yet, in their headlong rush to data science, big data, machine learning and artificial intelligence, too many companies have ignored 'Small Data'. This is a huge miss. Small data spells opportunity for both regular people and companies.

CASE STUDY
Small data is for factory workers

Machine operators at a paper mill were frustrated because they could get their equipment to work properly. Their requests for help from the maintenance department had fallen on deaf ears or worse. Responses like 'The equipment is fine; you just don't know how to operate it' made for a tense work environment.

Help came from a surprising source: a plant-wide effort to collect and utilize data for improvement. The operators collected and presented data on past and current performance of the equipment, leading the maintenance department to acknowledge the clear drop-off in performance. The equipment got the service it needed and quality and productivity promptly improved.

Small data projects involve teams of a handful of employees, addressing issues in their local workplaces using small data sets – hundreds of data points, not the millions or more used in big data projects. They are tightly focussed and utilize basic analytic methods that are accessible to all. As Figure 6.2 depicts, companies are loaded with potential small data projects. Roger Hoerl, whom I mentioned in the Introduction, and I estimate that a 40-person department should be able to complete 20 projects a year, with each project yielding a financial benefit of $10,000 to $250,000 annually.[9] (Roger provided the two case studies cited here.) And the cumulative benefits are enormous.

CASE STUDY
Small data is for CEOs

A CEO gets upset when they find out how much the company is spending on outside accounting resources. A team is chartered to look at the expenses and figure out how to reduce them without sacrificing financial oversight. Existing data focuses on total invoice amounts, without providing insight into the details of the services provided. To attack the problem, the team works out a way to address this gap and, with the new data, immediately sees a couple of important issues:

- high-level and high-cost accounting resources, including partners, have been used periodically, and

- vastly different rates have been paid to different accounting organizations for the same level of resource, e.g. senior accountant

Armed with this data, the team proposes a policy on outside accounting resources that standardizes rates, and requires CEO approval for the use of partners. More efficient and consistent use of external accounting services and substantial savings result. Best of all, the CEO is happy.

Benefits

According to Sting and Loch, 75 per cent of the productivity gains at leading companies came from bottom-up ideas from regular people.[10] Unlike big data projects, which often involve dozens of people with disparate agendas, politics, enormous budgets and high failure rates, the probability of success is high.

The benefits continue. Like data quality, small data projects build the organizational data muscle that helps the entire company learn what it takes to succeed with data, gain needed skills, build confi-

FIGURE 6.2 Size of data required versus count of opportunities

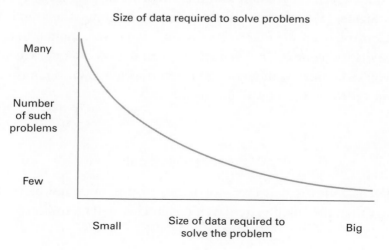

dence and breed the kind of culture that big data demands. And with many people worried that they will be replaced by automation or that their jobs will change in ways beyond their control, participating in these projects enables them to take proactive steps to build their skills and deal with their own fears.

Plus, they are fun! I find that most people revel in understanding the numbers, what they mean, and the detective work to sort out what is really going on. They love working on teams and seeing the results of their labour improve their work and their company's performance.

Once people know where to look, they don't have much trouble finding small data opportunities. Three 'target rich' areas include:

1 Reducing wasted time: people waste a lot of time, waiting for meetings to start, for inputs from a colleague, for a shipment to arrive, and so forth. The goal is to reduce that time.

2 Simplifying hand-offs: as work proceeds into, across and out of your team, poor hand-offs may increase complexity, cost or time. The goal is to streamline these hand-offs.

3 Data quality (from Chapter 5): most improvement projects require only small amounts of data.

One important note to conclude this discussion. I've provided more details, including a worked example, on completing a small data project in Toolkit D. There are plenty of other good methods: Six Sigma, Lean and Process Management enthusiasts have developed versions specifically tailored to the problems they address. Thus the Six Sigma DMAIC methodology combines some steps and adds C-Control, to ensure that a process, once improved, is put into a state of statistical control. In this respect, small data is a bit more general. If you're familiar with any good method to use data to improve the team's performance, by all means use it.

Make better decisions

The basic idea is that everyone learns to use more and better data today than they used yesterday, more and better data tomorrow than they used today – and so on into the future – in order to make better decisions. This is the essence of becoming data-driven. But so far, the most outstanding feature surrounding 'data-driven decision-making' is the hype – I don't know of a single company that has made it a dominant strategy or even a dominant feature of their data programme. This is somewhat paradoxical – all companies strive to make better decisions. And sooner or later, making better decisions will become a must-do for regular people (see Chapter 3).

The good news is that regular people don't have to wait around for their companies to decide better decision-making is important. You can systematically evaluate and improve your own decision-making using the steps outlined in Toolkit E.

Informationalize products and services

Here the idea is to build more data into an existing product or service to make it more valuable. The concept builds on the notion of 'the right data' to better meet a customer's needs. While my favourite example is the beer can that changes colour when the contents are the right temperature to drink, there are hundreds of such examples.[11] Older drivers tease that their car dashboards now resemble a fighter pilot's cockpit, telling them how far they can go on the fuel remaining, directions, tyre pressure, and so forth. For example, most people don't spend much time interpreting graphics, but even something as basic as a time-series plot can be informationalized. For example, the 'good this way' pointer helps the reader of Figure 6.3 to draw proper conclusions.

Informationalizing a product can create new business opportunities.[12] For example, Sleep Number has informationalized its mattresses by building in sensors that track heart rates and breathing patterns, helping the company identify chronic sleep issues and enabling it to expand its scope to wellness. Caterpillar employs sensors in its heavy machinery to collect data that will help it predict failures – and get into the maintenance business.

FIGURE 6.3 Making graphs easier to interpret

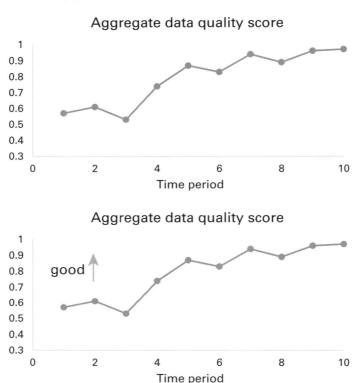

No matter who you are, you can almost certainly make your products and services more valuable by informationalizing them. And, as the examples in the last paragraph illustrate, you may be able to grow revenue. Thus, every person, team and company should very seriously consider informationalization at an important business strategy.

Exploit asymmetries and/or close them
(finance professionals and strategists)

To illustrate the main idea, consider pricing, a subject that has been top-of-mind for both buyers and sellers since time immemorial. In any transaction, the side that knows the most has an advantage.

Thus, a used-car dealer, who sees thousands of cars every year, simply knows more and is in a better position to know the 'fair price'. Since the buyer doesn't, the seller can inflate the prices at which they offer to sell the car, to their advantage. Online sales amplify this asymmetry, particularly if the seller can infer something about willingness to pay from the prospect's online searches.

The converse strategy is to close asymmetries. Consumer Reports is a classic example. Today, 'fact-checkers' serve incredibly important roles in keeping politicians and other public figures honest.

Unfortunately, in many cases, price checkers are not available. Any buyers, most of them anyway, do not wish to set themselves up as easy prey. They discount the seller's claims, effectively reducing the price they are willing to pay and reducing the value of the item for sale. So, closing the asymmetry is in everyone's interest. Here blockchain can help. For digital art, a Non-Fungible Token (NFT) can close much of the asymmetry associated with the provenance of the piece. In commercial real estate, locking every tax re-evaluation, every repair, every inspection, etc, into a blockchain as those events occur can do much to close the asymmetry. As Patrick O'Meara, CEO at Inveniam explained, 'There is a lot of commercial real estate out there. If a blockchain can increase the value of properties by even a few per cent, it would be a boon for investors.'[13]

Exploit proprietary data (product managers, strategists)

Perhaps the best business strategy of all involves having something no one else does and exploiting it. Almost all companies have data that no other company has. For example, you alone possess the sequence of customer transactions between your company and your customers. Proprietary data can be big or small, structured or unstructured, raw or refined – the key feature is not easily replicated by another company. Good examples include S&P's CUSIP, which uniquely identify securities, Facebook's friends data, and GM Cruise Automation's maps and sensor data.[14,15]

Potential value aside, I still see very few organizations that give proprietary data its due, or that have complete plans for how to acquire, develop and leverage it. Those that do concentrate too much on their internal data, which may be proprietary, but which does not achieve its full potential value until it is combined with external data.

As Tom Davenport and myself opine, the need for proprietary data strategies is increasing with new data types and the growth of artificial intelligence (AI). There are many new types of data emerging across industries – sensor data, mobile data, new types of payment data, and more. Most commercial AI involves machine learning, and if your company has the same data as everyone else, it will have the same models informing these models and predictions – and thus no competitive advantage. Thus, organizations need to think about their proprietary data strategy and put it into action *now*.

Some companies and industries are already pointing the way to effective proprietary data strategy. Alphabet's Waymo and GM's Cruise Automation, for example, are assiduously gathering maps and sensor data from billions of miles of simulated and on-road driving. Firms focussed on medical imaging for AI-assisted radiology or pathology are acquiring or partnering for image data. Companies in media assiduously protect the value of their films, TV series, news, books, magazines, and so forth, and are increasingly distributing those content assets in a variety of formats and channels, many of which are envisioned at the beginning of a content creation project.

Strategic data science (senior leaders)

One category of small data science projects is especially important – strategic data science.[16] To illustrate, consider two options at a mid-sized media company. Option 1 involves looking for insights that deepen the user experience using data generated by engagement with its apps. Option 2 involves using data to inform a bid for certain licensing rights, something that comes up every couple of years. There is plenty of data in support of Option 1 – it is certainly important. But although there is relatively little data in support of Option 2, it is strategic. Bidding too low and losing can do immediate and long-term harm; bidding too high takes away from profit.

The small quantity of data aside, a senior data scientist can add enormous value: from helping ensure the problem is clearly stated; to analysing what small data is available, coming up with better insights, and quantifying uncertainty; to searching for new sources of data, including proposing experiments to do so; to creating great graphics; to calling out minimizing hidden biases and groupthink; and aligning disparate points of view. Senior leaders are regular people too and they should seek out the company's most experienced data scientist for such efforts. Conversely, data scientists should do more of this work.

Treat customer privacy as a feature (privacy professionals)

To date, most companies have taken a rather defensive posture with respect to consumer privacy. Their chief protection officers are lawyers and they ask potential consumers to agree to long, arcane statements to even browse a website. I suppose this makes some sense – after all potential GDPR fines are scary indeed.

Still, erecting barriers for potential customers never seems like a good idea. While many people don't seem to care much about privacy, a small cadre of desirable (younger, richer, more tech-savvy) consumers do.[17] For these people, privacy appears to be as much about customer experience as anything else.

So I wonder, what would happen if a company adopted a different approach, viewing privacy as a feature inherent to their brand, providing simple, clear explanations of policy, and using privacy to distinguish itself from its competitors? I know of no company that has done so. An opportunity for some marketing professional to distinguish their company from others!

It is telling that companies routinely seek consumers' feedback regarding their products and services, yet do not ask them about privacy. So one way to start is talking directly with customers about their expectations and their openness to your new ideas and what they view as fair compensation for your use of their data.

A good second idea is simplifying and shortening your privacy policies in ways that build trust – not the long-winded boilerplate that most companies subject people to. Clarify the compensation customers and users may expect in exchange for their data – whether in money, discounts, or services – and make it easier to opt in or out.

Third, while one should expect the privacy landscape to change rapidly and chaotically over the next several years, now might be a good time to think long term. Years ago, when I worked at Bell Labs, an unknown prognosticator opined that, 'Privacy will be to the Information Age as product safety was to the Industrial Age.' This individual observed that, over time, societies came to expect companies to produce safe products. Both legal and market pressures came to bear. In some cases, these protections may have gone too far – is it really necessary to warn coffee drinkers, 'Caution, contents may be hot'? But right or wrong, that is how society 'voted'.

So ask yourself these questions: Do you think there is wisdom in the prediction? Do you have a different one? Finally, how do you want to position your company and its brand with respect to privacy over the long term? As you puzzle through these questions, I think you will see many opportunities to embrace data privacy in ways that distinguish you from others.

Get data on the balance sheet (finance professionals)

One interesting and important property of data is that it is an abstraction, and therefore largely invisible. And it is harder to manage that which you can't see. Thus, at some high level, most people will agree that 'data', some of it anyway, is an asset (conversely, at some high level, most people will agree that bad data is a liability). These observations lead some to the mantra, 'manage your data as assets'. Still, in the absence of any tangible measurement, it is hard to know what to do.

One way to resolve this issue is to get data on the balance sheet. The finance professional who sorts out which of these to use and how to make it work will do an enormous service to their company in ways that are not yet fleshed out. For example, the data may serve as collateral backing a loan, it may make the data more saleable, or it may simply inspire management to pay greater attention. Laney, in his book *Infonomics,* offers six ways that finance professionals can approach this opportunity.[18]

Explore the many other ways to put data to work

It turns out there are many other ways for companies to put data to work giving both regular people and companies many options. Here I simply mention four, urging people and companies to give each some consideration, to expand their thinking about the range of possibilities, and to get their creative juices flowing.[19]

Provide new data/content

A generation ago, the obvious example of a provider of new content would have been the newspaper. Now there are many more original sources. And not just for the news. Noom, for example, provides customized diet and exercise regimens, far beyond anything in standard regimens.

Repackage existing data

In contrast to developers of new content, repackagers don't focus on creating new content, but on packaging it up in different ways. Facebook is a great example.

Unbundle data from products and services

The converse of informationalizing is unbundling. For travel agents, whose fees were built into the prices of the fares, accommodations and tours they booked, this has proven essential, as many clients can now do their own bookings. Travel agents are becoming 'advisors', charging for their advice and expertise separately.

Infomediate

Infomediators don't create new data per se, but make it easier for those seeking information to find it. Google is the perfect example.

Most important takeaways

- While big data and artificial intelligence garner the lion's share of interest, the lion's share of opportunity lies in small data (including strategic data science). For most companies, small data should be their second focus, once they have traction with quality.
- All companies should attempt to sort out opportunities to exploit their proprietary data.
- Companies should develop a fuller understanding of the many other ways to put data to work and, in time, develop a plan to take advantage of those best suited to their overall business strategies. All depend on regular people, so companies should get them involved as soon as possible.
- There have never been more opportunities for regular people to carve out a niche for themselves.
- Data is a team sport. Even the most esoteric big data project requires contributions from a variety of regular people if it is to create value.

Notes

1 The figure I've used here comes from: R Kenett and TC Redman (2019) *The Real Work of Data Science: Turning data into information, better decisions, and stronger organizations*, Wiley. Ron is responsible for the original sequence of steps – I've made some minor modifications to shorten the process here.

2 TC Redman. Are you setting your data scientists up to fail?, *Harvard Business Review*, 25 January 2018, hbr.org/2018/01/are-you-setting-your-data-scientists-up-to-fail (archived at https://perma.cc/FF2L-VRQB)

3 I first published a version of this table in: TC Redman. Your data initiatives can't just be for data scientists, *Harvard Business Review*, 22 March 2022, hbr.org/2022/03/your-data-initiatives-cant-just-be-for-data-scientists (archived at https://perma.cc/U6PK-E3BQ)

4 A Augereau. Data + Design, JP Morgan, www.youtube.com/watch?v=Ku8x1ina_N4 (archived at https://perma.cc/X3RM-7CSS)

5 A Ettore. How Disney uses data to skyrocket its business #35, LinkedIn, www.linkedin.com/pulse/how-disney-uses-analytics-skyrocket-its-business-35-ettorre-mba/?trk=eml-email_series_follow_newsletter_01-hero-1-title_link&midToken=AQFykt2dOEr3gQ&fromEmail=fromEmail&ut=0y64DA12C2R9I1 (archived at https://perma.cc/9RSB-2NRW)

6 Y Atsmon, T Saleh, S Nair, P Jain, S Kishore and B McCarthy. Tipping the scales in AI: How leaders capture exponential returns, McKinsey, 23 April 2021, www.mckinsey.com/industries/technology-media-and-telecommunications/our-insights/tipping-the-scales-in-ai?cid=other-eml-dre-mip-mck&hlkid=a774e1a8976d4a078406df70a8406fd5&hctky=11750595&hdpid=e87f8985-f192-42f9-998f-175d4bba9560 (archived at https://perma.cc/UQU4-APQJ)

7 T Davenport. The shift to collaborative analytics, Forbes.com, 30 April 2021

8 Email communication of 28 January 2021

9 R Snee and R Hoerl (2018) *Leading Holistic Improvement with Lean Six Sigma 2.0*, Pearson FT Press

10 FJ Sting and CH Loch. Implementing operations strategy: How vertical and horizontal coordination interact, *Production and Operations Management*, December 2015, 25 (7), 1177–193, onlinelibrary.wiley.com/doi/abs/10.1111/poms.12537 (archived at https://perma.cc/V4NW-Q32L)

11 TC Redman. Integrate data into your products or get left behind, *Harvard Business Review*, 28 June 2012, hbr.org/2012/06/integrate-data-in-products-or-get (archived at https://perma.cc/V8Y6-6WWT)

12 M Subramaniam. How smart products create connected customers, *Sloan Management Review*, Autumn 2022, 33–37

13 Personal communication with Patrick O'Meara, 31 October 2022

14 For examples (see also note 15): T Davenport and T Redman. Your organization needs a proprietary data strategy, *Harvard Business Review*, 4 May 2020, hbr.org/2020/05/your-organization-needs-a-proprietary-data-strategy (archived at https://perma.cc/NWE7-X48W)

15 T Redman. Invest in proprietary data for competitive advantage, *Harvard Business Review*, 28 March 2013, blogs.hbr.org/2013/03/invest-in-proprietary-data-for/ (archived at https://perma.cc/2J86-G6VJ)

16 TC Redman and TH Davenport. Four ways to democratize data science in your organization, *Harvard Business Review*, 8 March 2021, store.hbr.org/product/4-ways-to-democratize-data-science-in-your-organization/H068AY (archived at https://perma.cc/2TYG-PSCV)

17 TC Redman and R Waitman. Do you care about privacy as much as your customers do?, *Harvard Business Review*, 28 January 2020, hbr.org/2020/01/do-you-care-about-privacy-as-much-as-your-customers-do (archived at https://perma.cc/JCS5-JPRP)

18 DB Laney (2018) *Infonomics: How to monetize, manage and measure information as an asset for competitive advantage*, Bibliomotion Inc

19 I've selected these from: discussions with Doug Laney, author of *Infonomics* (see note 18); and from TC Redman (2008) *Data Driven: Profiting from your most important business asset*, Harvard Business School Press

PART THREE

Data is a team sport

7

Fat organizational pipes

Regular people can't solve all problems

Recall Figure 3.1 from Chapter 3 which described the people and organizational structures needed to get everyone involved and make data a team sport. The most neglected feature has been regular people at the centre of the figure; and the second most neglected the fat organizational pipes needed to connect everyone up. These pipes are on the figure's periphery and the subject of this chapter (see Figure 7.1).

FIGURE 7.1 Components of a better organization for data

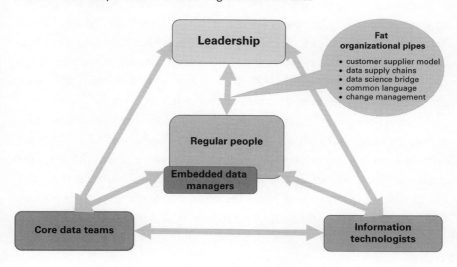

The unfortunate reality is that organizations erect barriers that make executing the 'data is a team sport' mantra more difficult. It is easy to cite 'silos, silos, silos', and this is a decent one-word description of the problem. But some critical issues go deeper. The first sections of this chapter explore them in detail. Make no mistake – these are deep fundamental problems! Then we'll discuss five varieties of 'fat organizational pipes' as the best means available to deal with the issues. 'Organizational pipes' because they connect people (an analogy to technical pipes, by which the data actually flows) and 'fat' because they facilitate high-bandwidth, multi-way communications.

The suffocating effects of silos

While I have no hard metric, I find that most people enjoy working with people outside their departments. They enjoy the interactions, the process of sorting out how to work together to attack problems, the freedom that doing so brings, the sheer joy in working together to solve a long-standing problem, and the empowerment that comes from the experience.

Yet, left on their own, most people retreat to their silos. Even after a successful project! This is unfortunate because silos are the enemy of the teamwork companies need to truly leverage their data. Recall Stephanie from Chapter 5. Even in the simplest possible situation, she did not reach across departmental lines to make a connection. Silos do not form hermetically sealed data barriers, but they do make many things in the data space more difficult.

These issues grow larger as more coordination is required. Consider a data product such as a financial report. Producing such a report requires compiling and synthesizing data created in the various departments. Producing the actual report is easy compared to the effort needed to clean and align the data. More silos mean exponentially more work... and more opportunities for things to go wrong.

Silos present even bigger problems for data science, as there is a hidden, designed-in tension between business and data science teams that get in the way.[1] To explain, I'll use the metaphor of a 'factory' and a data science 'lab'. 'The factory' may literally be a factory, but it could also be a business operation that produces decisions on mortgage applications, reads MRIs or drills oil wells.

Factory goals include meeting production plans and keeping unit costs low. The watchword is stability: no major disruptions and no surprises. Factory managers must work very hard to establish and maintain stability, so, naturally, they resist anything that threatens it (one important exception is that good factory managers support small data projects and the incremental improvements they bring, provided these efforts are driven by the factory).

The data science lab, on the other hand, is specifically designed to disrupt the factory. Its job is to find bigger improvements than can be made with small data in the factory, to change the way decisions are made, and to come up with new products that obviate old ones. The lab represents the very antithesis of stability – exactly the sorts of things that factory managers hate!

To be clear, a certain amount of friction between any two departments is to be expected. After all, they compete for budget, people and senior attention. All things being equal, factory managers prefer to be left alone to do their jobs. They certainly do not appreciate interference from Finance when it changes accounting practices, or from HR when it mandates improvements to its employee review system. But these are mere annoyances; they don't fundamentally change the way the factory works. Contrast these annoyances with the full-frontal attack and disruption signalled by the lab.

Note that this tension is 'designed in' as there is considerable value in separating business operations from the data team (see the box 'Is this on Edison').[2] An emphasis on stability in operations keeps costs low. An emphasis on long-term, disruptive work by the data team is essential to foster innovation and future success. But these divergent goals create tensions that threaten data science!

IS THIS ON EDISON?

Thomas Edison is generally recognized as launching the world's first industrial research lab in Menlo Park, New Jersey, in the late 19th century. As my co-authors Roger Hoerl and Diego Kuonen and others have observed, Edison seems to have recognized that embedding lab resources into a factory would not work, as those assigned are quickly pulled into day-in, day-out stability issues. After all, maintaining stability is hard and new issues crop up constantly. The net effect is to thwart true invention. Conversely, separating the lab from the factory risks isolating the lab and turning it into the proverbial 'ivory tower'.

Edison was able to mitigate the tension because he led both the lab and the factory. But for most other organizations since then, this ongoing tension has never been adequately resolved.

Lack of common language also makes working together more difficult

The second major barrier to the teamwork data requires is lack of common language. While most people don't think about it, common language is essential to their businesses. Companies and others employ standards to ensure that a metre is the same length worldwide, calendars ensure that everyone shows up for meetings at the same time, and everyone agrees what 'payment in US dollars' means. It is trite, but no less important, to note that without some common language, commerce would be impossible.

Still, it is the exception. Consider the pandemic. Good information is potentially our best weapon in fighting coronavirus, but there are no common definitions of terms as basic as 'death due to coronavirus'.[3] Lives are lost and people suffer unnecessarily.

Fortunately, most issues are more mundane, though many of them are significant. Managers struggle to answer basic questions like 'How many customers do we have?' for their bosses because different business units have different definitions of 'customer'. Lack of common language makes it even more difficult for managers to coordinate work across departmental silos, and technologists spend more time dealing with 'systems that don't talk' than they do implementing new technologies. Most of the added effort needed to accommodate the lack of common language has become so embedded in work life that, like other data quality issues, people don't even notice it.

To establish and maintain common language, it is important to understand how disparate language takes root and grows. First, the seeds of disparate language are sewn as businesses grow, change and innovate, naturally leading teams and departments to develop and adopt new, increasingly specialized business language to help them do their work efficiently. To illustrate this point, consider that *customer* comes to mean distinctly different things to different departments quite naturally: to Marketing it means 'qualified prospect', to Sales it means 'the person with sign-off authority', and to Finance it is 'whoever is responsible for paying the bill'. In the context of the entire company, *customer* has three different legitimate meanings, while each department focuses on only one.

This may not have presented much of an issue when the company was small – or when there was plenty of person-to-person communication across department lines. After all, most people can tolerate a certain amount of ambiguity. And, unconsciously perhaps, they know common language is important. We all say things like, 'Let's make sure we're not comparing apples to oranges' or 'Let's make sure we are on the same page' to make sure we are in sync with others. (But not always. One of the most brutal political spats I observed unfolded when two departments pushed forward different numbers for MARKET SHARE. The issue was only resolved when a junior staffer noticed that the two employed different definitions. Even so, both sides had good reasons for their definitions and were hesitant to change!)

The situation grows worse as departments automate their work. They use computer systems and applications, which employ *data models* and *databases* to capture and lock in the business language of their users. While automation can help each department boost efficiency, it also means that disparate language winds up in disparate, department-level databases.

Exacerbating this, computers don't deal with ambiguity as well as people. They don't care what terms mean and lock in inconsistent definitions. In particular, each department builds the role it sees for *customer* into its departmental database. One visible result of this problem is that management can't get a clear answer to the aforementioned 'how many customers do we have?' Further, it is increasingly difficult for departments to share data in meaningful ways.

Less visible is the work people must do to accommodate these disparate systems; business departments develop work-arounds and IT crafts custom interfaces to connect these systems. These measures add complexity, though without them, work would halt. (NOTE: the totality of these disparate systems, added software to accommodate them, and added work performed to work around them constitute *technical debt*. It will continue to grow until companies erect some guardrails to prevent the unfettered growth of disparate language. I'll discuss technical debt further in Chapter 8.)

Complicating matters still further, the issues and opportunities that would benefit from common language do not announce themselves as such. Thus, when people complain that 'our systems don't talk', they mis-diagnose the issue as computer-related and assign it to their tech departments. But 'systems not talking' stems directly from the lack of common language, which tech departments cannot establish.

There are a few bad actors

One question that always comes up as companies start their data programmes is 'who owns the data?' Almost everyone comes up with some version of the right answer, which is, 'Data is a company asset. Unless there are special concerns, everyone should have access to the data they need.' The special concerns may include sensitive data, privacy restrictions and security regulations.

If only it were that simple! For a few people act as though they truly own the data. They may simply refuse to share, take steps to hide the existence of potentially useful data from others, or impose arduous terms under which they will share – so arduous as to drive potential customers away. I call these people 'active resistors'. I really don't blame such people – after all data conveys power.

Importantly, sharing data is hard work. If your neighbour asks to borrow your rake, you'll probably let them. If they ask to borrow your lawn-mower, you will probably let them also, offering to show them how to charge the battery and start it up. Things are more complicated with data. All data is subtle and nuanced, specifically defined to designed to serve specific purposes. It may prove useful for some other purposes, but not for others. It takes a long time to explain all this to someone who wants to use your data. I call people who are happy to share the data but won't spare the time ensuring the 'sharee' can use it effectively 'passive resistors'. I really don't blame such people either – sharing data is hard and not in the job description!

Even as their motivations differ, the end result is that the data is not shared.

Do away with silos?

It is tempting to conclude that companies should do away with silos. Companies can organize themselves in any way they want: 'horizon-tally' around business processes, around key people, as loose confederations of experts that come together to solve specific prob-lems, and so forth.

But I don't think silos are going away any time soon. There will be advantages and disadvantages, however a company organizes itself. Silos stem from the concept of 'division of labour' – a key idea in industrialization that has contributed to enormous productivity gains for over 150 years. On the factory floor, division of labour meant one worker hung the doors, another bolted on the tyres, and a third installed the windows. An assembly line coordinated their work. Costs went down, production and wages went up! Silos make top-down management easier, and from a data perspective, they do offer one extremely important advantage: people working within them develop a deep understanding of the data needed to do their work. Silos have done, and still do, a lot of good.[4]

These advantages aside, silos are still a big problem when it comes to data. The best way to address them is with 'fat organizational pipes'. They make it possible to bridge silos, make it easier for regular people to connect and to share data, enable the 'data is a team sport' mantra and develop common language issues discussed here.

The 'pipes' come in four mutually reinforcing varieties, and include:

1 The customer–supplier model, which helps data creators, data customers, and possibly others connect. It is nothing more than the well-known customer–supplier model, one of the most powerful management insights ever, applied to data.

2 Data supply chain management, which builds on the customer–supplier model for long, complex flows of data.

3 The data science bridge, aimed at addressing the special problems silos present for data science.

4 Common language, which aims to ensure that, when people or computer systems 'talk', they share a vocabulary.

I also include 'change management' as a fifth organizational pipe, though it is somewhat different. There is no question that the changes called for here are massive. Proactively managing that change is essential.

We'll explore how each works in this chapter and summarize senior management's roles in setting up them up in Chapter 9.

The customer–supplier model

I view the customer–supplier model, presented in Figure 7.2, as the most important tool in all of data.[5] It puts regular people/their teams/their process/their department/their company in the middle, recognizing their roles as data creators and customers.

To the right are customers and other stakeholders – those who receive and use your stuff. (NOTE: While our primary interest is data, please interpret 'stuff' quite generally to include technology, physical products, services, and anything else that leaves your company, including pollution, defects and misinformation.) To the left are suppliers, those on whom you depend. The left-to-right arrows represent the primary flow of data, products and services.

Finally, the right-to-left flows are the requirements and feedback (e.g. communications) channels that are so necessary if the teamwork called for here is to have any chance. As an advisor, I first look to see whether such channels exist, whether they work properly, and whether they are staffed by people held accountable that they do so. In most cases, they do not. Said differently, most fall into the 'Stephanie trap'.

People must build the right-to-left communications channels. Doing so is easier than it might appear and makes rapid data quality improvements possible. It also makes automating the left-to-right flows of data easier and more effective.

One company that employed the customer–supplier model to advantage is Altria, the US-based provider of tobacco and smoke-free products. Altria depends on point-of-sale data from over 100,000 convenience stores daily to complete its market reports and analysis. A team reporting to Kirby Forlin, VP Advanced Analytics, manages this base. Data requirements are spelled out in contracts and the team aims to help stores meet them. To begin, Altria concentrated on its

FIGURE 7.2 Connecting data creators and customers via the customer–supplier model

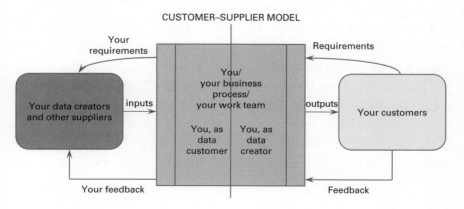

most basic requirements. Quality was poor, with only 58 per cent of daily submissions meeting them. But the Altria team worked patiently, improving quality to 98 per cent in three years. As the score for basic quality improved, the Altria team added its more advanced requirements to the mix. As Forlin noted, 'This is a work in progress. The evidence that we can increasingly trust the data saves us a lot of work in our analytics practice and builds trust into our work.'[6]

Data supply chain management[7]

Now the story becomes more complex. Companies have always produced complex data products in the form of financial statements, reports to regulators, projected sales reports, and so forth. The range and importance of such products is growing as, for examples, data science teams seek to embed analytics and AI-derived models into products that serve both internal and external customers. Morgan Stanley's Next Best Action is a good example.

Producing such products means pulling together often disparate data from across the company, and, increasingly, outside the company. Actually assembling the report is child's play compared to acquiring trustworthy data, where all the issues discussed throughout this book come into play. As already noted, chief financial officers tell me that upwards of three-quarters of their staff's time is spent dealing with mundane data issues. Data scientists have invented the term 'data wrangling' to describe the work needed to make data fit for their use. It consumes up to 80 per cent of the effort.

Data product managers have fallen into a larger, more sinister version of the 'Stephanie trap', making themselves responsible for the quality of data they do not create.

Fortunately, there is a better way to source high-quality data. It builds on the customer–supplier model and process, and the supplier management techniques used by manufacturers of physical products. In particular, manufacturers extend deep into their supply chains to clarify their requirements, qualify suppliers, insist that suppliers measure quality, and make needed improvements at the source(s) of problem(s). This enables them to assemble components into finished products with minimal 'physical product wrangling', improving quality and lowering costs.

Data supply chain management puts equal emphasis on all aspects of data management — from sorting out what customers require, to determining what data is needed, to ensuring that such data is created correctly, to organizing that data, to assembly of data products. It's a means of balancing the benefits of common data with those of unique and tailored data in products (see the box 'An under-appreciated complication'), and it's equally suited to internal and external data.

AN UNDER-APPRECIATED COMPLICATION

Many data science projects and data products 'repurpose' data created for another purpose. For example, a clothing manufacturer uses sales data to deliver product to customers. This data is then repurposed for use in sales and financial reports. Such repurposing complicates quality management. For example, no one expects a starter designed for a Ford Explorer to fit into a Subaru Outback. We don't yet understand the full implications!

There is a simple elegance to data supply chain management, so I've included a short summary of the steps as Tool F. Of special interest here is Step 1: Establish Management Responsibilities. In consists of two sub-steps:

a. The product manager names a 'data supply chain manager' to coordinate the effort and recruits a team from each department, including external data sources, across the supply chain. Embedded data managers (see Chapter 10) are great candidates.

b. Put issues associated with data sharing and ownership front and centre. Most issues melt away, as few managers wish to take a hard stance against data sharing in front of their peers.

While not enough companies employ data supply chain management, those that do report solid results. For example, AT&T, which pioneered the method, used the method to improve financial assurance, saving itself and the industry about a quarter of a billion dollars per year.[8]

The data science bridge

The data science bridge[9] adapts the customer–suppler model to deal with the special rigours silos impose on data science, as discussed earlier. To extend the 'factory/lab' metaphor, imagine that the factory and lab sit on opposite sides of a river. A bridge spans the river and connects the two, resolving the essential strains between the two and enabling the introduction of more, and more useful, data-driven innovations into the factory.

A data science bridge has four major responsibilities:

1 **Developing and maintaining high-bandwidth, bi-directional communications channels between the factory and the lab.** This includes developing a common vocabulary (so the factory and lab don't talk past one another), identifying and clarifying which innovations are most needed (so the lab focuses on the right things), and ensuring feedback is provided and understood.

2 **Developing and operating a process by which lab inventions are made fit for the factory.** This may include embedding newly minted algorithms into factory technologies and/or IT systems, training factory employees and so on.

3 **Selecting and allocating needed resources.** People and funding would be assigned to prioritized innovative opportunities.

4 **Building trust between the factory, the lab and senior management.** Ultimately, only trust can mitigate the tension.

Tool H provides a flowchart which describes how the bridge does this work.

There are forerunners to the bridge in a technology transfer process that connected Bell Labs and AT&T a generation ago;[10] more generic D4 ('Data, Discovery, Delivery, Dollars') processes;[11] and the 'analytics translators who stand between technical and business organizations'.[12] Today, the Federal Statistical Office in Switzerland is showing the way in building the bridge as part of its Data Science Competence Centre. While it is still early days, Diego Kuonen, who is helping build it, noted that the bridge is taking chaos out of the previous process. He observed:

> Most important decisions are taken on the bridge. It has facilitated 'communities of practice', which are providing real benefits in the 'factory'.

Still Kuonen is philosophical. 'I think we're only scratching the surface,' he observed. 'Common language is really hard. We need to get that right.'

Of course, few other organizations are that far along. So most should start by developing an operational definition of 'data science' (or 'AI', 'analytics' or whatever name the lab goes by) and asking some preliminary questions:

- What current lab projects would most benefit from better business connections?
- Which factory teams needs to be connected first? Which lab teams?
- Are there candidates to lead the bridge from within the factory or lab who are respected enough by the other function to be effective?
- How do we align the bridge to the company's strategic interests?

Next, the leader of the data science lab, who in many cases has the most to gain, should initiate dialogue with a factory leader. Initially, a 'footbridge' or informal connector between the lab and factory may suffice. Open-minded lab and factory leaders can take the initiative to discuss the concept across organizational boundaries, and go to senior leadership with specific proposals.

Lower-level managers and technical resources do not need to wait for top-down direction, either. They can certainly identify areas within their own departments where the tension between the lab and the factory is inhibiting progress and begin a dialogue to discuss how to foster better cooperation.

Establishing and maintaining common language

Common language makes it easier to pursue all work, goals and strategies that *require coordinated action,* including delivery products and services, evaluating business opportunities, responding to threats, reducing technical debt, sharing data, and building a platform for a data-driven future. Even better, a carefully developed and deployed common language will serve an organization in good stead for a very long time.[13]

The International Finance Corporation developed a common language to reconcile operational and financial data and lessen the acrimony that respective departments felt towards one another.[14] US State Government Departments have developed common language to improve customer service and data quality and reduce development and ongoing expenses. Aera Energy LLC, a California-based oil and gas company, developed a common language to accelerate the implementation of standard processes across the company, to free up engineers and geoscientists to spend more time on technical analysis and decision-making, and to reduce technical debt.[15] Coordinated action across the entire telecommunications industry is required so two people can talk on their cell phones. Indeed, without standard protocols, the internet itself would collapse. Similarly, the need to make checkout faster, improve logistics, and improve customer service motivated the entire retail industry's interest in Universal Product Codes (e.g. barcodes), which uniquely identify each product's manufacturer and the product itself.[16]

These examples illustrate the numerous, potential *long-term* benefits to individuals, departments, companies and entire industries. Most pertinent here, those building their futures in data, data science and artificial intelligence must work in a coordinated fashion to share data, build models and make data-driven decisions. Smart businesses will smell opportunity and seek it out.

Still, of the five fat organizational pipes, common language is probably the most difficult to put in place. The two most important reasons appear to be:

- In the absence of an immediate problem, the short-term costs of developing a common language may exceed the short-term benefits, making it difficult to sustain the effort.

- Even under the best of circumstances, it takes a powerful combination of business urgency, long-term thinking, people, process and vision, to complete the work (see Tool H for a complete list of criteria).

Keys to advancing common language

There are several keys to surmounting these issues. First, as I previously noted, dealing with the lack of common language has become so entwined with day-to-day work that most people don't notice it. The first key is simply developing a feel for the problem. To do so, pick three or four common terms – for a financial services company, *security*, *buyer* and *client* are good examples – and ask people to write down their definitions of these terms. Pull them together on a sheet of paper and see how well they agree. Most find that the various definitions are far apart – when one regional bank conducted the exercise, they came up with over 20 distinct definitions for 'inactive customer'.

The unfortunate reality is that most efforts to create common language at the enterprise level fail. The second key is picking your spots. While reducing technical debt and departmental in-fighting are both worthy goals that common language may advance, assembling the coalition of people needed to do so may prove impossible for the former and eminently doable for the latter.

Senior leaders, and specifically a very senior Head of Common Language, must clarify exactly what problem is to be solved, weigh the potential benefits against the likelihood of failure (the criteria presented in Resource Centre 1 can help), and make an informed decision about moving forward.

The next key is to cut the problem down to size by focussing first on the concepts that bind the company. Recall the example above, where *customer* meant different things to different people. The secret to resolving the conflict lies in recognizing and elucidating the underlying concepts:[17]

1 First, treat 'prospects', 'signers' and 'responsible payers' not as tangible things, but as *roles* played by one or more persons or groups of persons (e.g. organizations).

2 Abstract a bit further, defining a 'party' as 'a person or organization of interest to the enterprise'.

3 Take advantage of the flexibility this permits, assigning as many *roles* to parties, as befits the business.

With this approach, a single concept, *party,* makes it easier for Marketing, Sales and Finance to work together, even as they focus on specific roles inside their respective departments. Experience shows that no more than 150 such concepts are sufficient to transform the entire company.[18]

The fourth key involves incorporating these concepts into data models and systems architectures and using judgement to enforce them. As a practical matter, this means allowing local variations when needed to solve specific problems and at the same time rigidly enforcing them at any higher level.

The final key is assembling a range of diverse talent. From abstract data modellers to those who can express complex thoughts clearly, to business managers, to technologists, to the just mentioned 'enforcers', to communicators (who sell the effort), to process managers whose job resembles 'herding cats' as much as anything else – there is no substitute for getting the right people involved.

Change management

The notion that regular people are both data creators and data customers is obvious, once one sees it. It is also transformational – establishing new working relationships on a company-wide scale changes everything! And it may be the least controversial of the organizational upgrades proposed here. The very notion that data presents unprecedented opportunity to regular people, the claim that small data is (today anyway) more important than big data, the need for common language, and the notion that people actually work together across silos – all will prove disruptive.

The promise of rich rewards aside, most people and companies have resisted and will continue to do so – either actively or passively – just as they resist all change. There is no sure remedy, but proactive, professional change management can help. It has been a big part of many of my clients' successes. Rather than attempting to summarize the rich literature on the subject, I'll simply present a figure (Figure 7.3) that has served me well and describe how I use it.[19]

As Figure 7.3 expresses, successful change requires that a lot happens in concert. Take away any of the four components and the effort fails to launch, fizzles, or worse. One way I use the figure is to help companies ensure they're not missing something that will trip them up, e.g.:

· Is this really a top three priority?

· Is the vision clear? More importantly, does everyone buy in?

FIGURE 7.3 A model for managing change

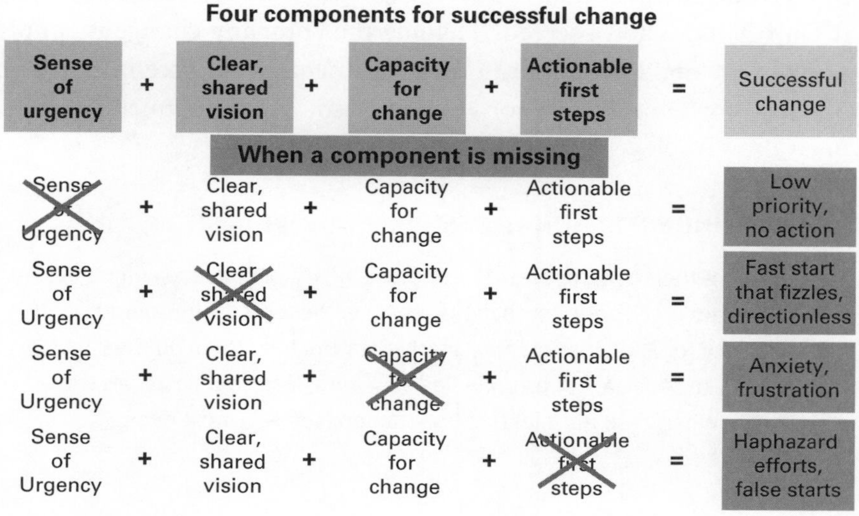

Four components for successful change

Sense of urgency	+	**Clear, shared vision**	+	**Capacity for change**	+
Actionable first steps	=	Successful change			

When a component is missing

~~Sense of Urgency~~ + Clear, shared vision + Capacity for change + Actionable first steps	=	Low priority, no action
Sense of Urgency + ~~Clear, shared vision~~ + Capacity for change + Actionable first steps	=	Fast start that fizzles, directionless
Sense of Urgency + Clear, shared vision + ~~Capacity for change~~ + Actionable first steps	=	Anxiety, frustration
Sense of Urgency + Clear, shared vision + Capacity for change + ~~Actionable first steps~~	=	Haphazard efforts, false starts

- Do we have the intellectual curiosity, the financial resources, the emotional resilience, and the courage needed make the needed changes?
- Do people know what they should do now?

There is almost always some area or other that commands attention.

Importantly, and especially pertinent to the main themes here, the figure is 'recursive', in that it applies at any level: from the personal, to the work team, to even the largest company or government agency. At the individual level, almost everyone can find things that are within their power to make better (that is, they have the capacity to change). I've emphasized data quality and small data (vision) and provided toolkits to help you get started (first steps). I've emphasized opportunity, but generally people have to find their own sense of urgency (as those joining the data generation have done).

The diagnosis grows increasingly complex the larger the team or company, though the emphasis on people, quality, small data, and steps to addressing silos highlight much of what must be done is a big start. (Ultimately, deep, fundamental change is top-down and unfortunately too many senior leaders have remained on the side-lines. I'll take that up in Chapter 9.)

Still, deeper expertise in change management is extremely helpful. If your Human Resources department has it, ask that they join the fun. One HR department that has such expertise is led by Salma AlHajjaj, at Gulf Bank, who observed, 'Helping the company change is simply part of our job.' I wish more HR departments would see it that way. (See the box 'Opportunity for Human Resources departments'.)

OPPORTUNITY FOR HUMAN RESOURCES DEPARTMENTS

A dominant theme in this book is 'opportunity', for people and companies. Data and the organizational changes proposed here present a special opportunity for HR departments. Clearly data can help them do their jobs better, but the special opportunity lies in helping lead change across the company. When I ask my clients if they can engage HR, most demur, viewing the department as filled with bureaucrats adding to their work loads, as pushing theories about employee engagement that don't square with their realities, as barely able to complete the tasks assigned to them, and as behind the curve on anything quantitative.

I hope HR departments will see opportunity here. Embrace data, build expertise in change management, and get in the game!

Most important takeaways

- Many factors impede the teamwork that fully putting data to work requires. While silos top the list, a lack of common language and a few bad actors, who behave as though they own the data, also get in the way.

- Still, silos aren't going away. So companies must build 'fat organizational pipes' to deal with silos. I include the customer–supplier model, data supply chain management, the data science bridge, common language and change management as the most important.

- There is nothing fancy, nor easy, in building and operating them. See 'How to set up and manage data supply chains', 'How to manage data science at the enterprise level', and 'How to evaluate whether you can successfully develop and promulgate common language' in the Toolkit to help guide your efforts.

Notes

1 RW Hoerl, D Kuonen and TC Redman. To succeed with data science, first build the 'bridge', *Sloan Management Review*, 22 October 2020, sloanreview.mit.edu/article/to-succeed-with-data-science-first-build-the-bridge/ (archived at https://perma.cc/8BSY-2MNK)

2 G McCormick. Thomas Edison's accomplishments go beyond the bulb to modern R&D, Redshift, 2 September 2021; also B Walsh. The making of America: Thomas Edison, *Time Magazine*, 23 June 2010

3   TD Davenport, AB Godfrey and TC Redman. To fight pandemics, we need better data, *Sloan Management Review*, 25 August 2020, sloanreview.mit.edu/article/to-fight-pandemics-we-need-better-data/ (archived at https://perma.cc/H588-B865)

4   See, for example: H Vantrappen and F Wirtz. Making silos work for your organization, *Harvard Business Review*, 1 November 2021, hbr.org/2021/11/making-silos-work-for-your-organization (archived at https://perma.cc/L7MZ-GJU5)

5   TC Redman (2016) *Getting in Front on Data: Who does what*, Technics Publications

6   TD Davenport, T Evgeniou and TC Redman. Your data supply chains are probably a mess. Here's how to fix them, *Harvard Business Review*, 24 June 2021, hbr.org/2021/06/data-management-is-a-supply-chain-problem (archived at https://perma.cc/E6JS-UUN7)

7   TD Davenport, T Evgeniou and TC Redman. Your data supply chains are probably a mess. Here's how to fix them, *Harvard Business Review*, 24 June 2021, hbr.org/2021/06/data-management-is-a-supply-chain-problem (archived at https://perma.cc/YAN3-DDKN)

8   TC Redman (2016) *Getting in Front on Data: Who does what*, Technics Publications

9   RW Hoerl, D Kuonen and TC Redman. To succeed with data science, first build the 'bridge', *Sloan Management Review*, 22 October 2020, sloanreview.mit.edu/article/to-succeed-with-data-science-first-build-the-bridge/ (archived at https://perma.cc/XS33-NBYK)

10   J Gertner (2013) *The Idea Factory: Bell Labs and the great age of American innovation*, Penguin

11   T Redman and W Sweeney. To work with data you need a lab and a factory, *Harvard Business Review*, 4 April 2013, hbr.org/2013/04/two-departments-for-data-succe (archived at https://perma.cc/7QNS-2UYR)

12   N Henke, J Levine and P McInerney. You don't have to be a data scientist to fill this must-have analytics role, *Harvard Business Review*, 5 February 2018, hbr.org/2018/02/you-dont-have-to-be-a-data-scientist-to-fill-this-must-have-analytics-role (archived at https://perma.cc/P887-RQEW)

13   This section is based on work completed by a study group composed of myself, Dave Hay, C Lwanga Yonke and John Zachman. The group has published two research reports and a management summary (see notes 14–16)

14   D Hay, CL Yonke, TC Redman and J Zachman. The business case for common language: Not 'if' but 'what and when?', The Data Administration Newsletter, 16 December 2020, tdan.com/the-business-case-for-a-common-language-not-if-but-what-and-when/27617 (archived at https://perma.cc/NQU4-JBDM)

15 D Hay, CL Yonke, TC Redman and J Zachman. Developing and adopting a common language: What's required from an organizational perspective, The Data Administration newsletter, 1 April 2020, tdan.com/developing-and-adopting-a-common-language/26284 (archived at https://perma.cc/SA36-HTPN)

16 D Hay, CL Yonke, TC Redman and J Zachman. Effective digital transformation depends on common language, *Harvard Business Review*, 14 December 2021, hbr.org/2021/12/effective-digital-transformation-relies-on-a-shared-language (archived at https://perma.cc/F3TU-PCGX)

17 DC Hay (1996) *Data Model Patterns: Conventions of thought*, Dorset House Publishing Co

18 Discovering and articulating the 150 or so key concepts that underpin a company is incredibly hard work. Most need specialized help. In some cases, good industry models can jumpstart the work

19 I first learned of this figure some 30 years ago, when I was at AT&T. I do not know the source

8

Don't confuse apples and oranges

Great data programmes need great tech,
but there are massive contradictions

Companies need solid information technologies, IT departments and programmes if they are to implement and scale their data programmes. Yet, as the technology force field analysis presented in Chapter 2 illustrates, there are massive contradictions:

- On the one hand, as I've already noted, 'data' and 'information technology' are different sorts of assets that should be managed separately:

  - On the other hand, too many people and companies co-mingle management of the two, to the detriment of both, and the company. This contradiction manifests itself in any number of ways: sources of value are missed, IT gets saddled with data issues it cannot handle, and the hope that newer technology or transformation will mean better data is not met.

- On the one hand, there is considerable interest in digital transformation, particularly after Zoom and other technologies helped companies navigate the pandemic. Further, there is enormous potential in new technologies such as 'the cloud', artificial intelligence, blockchain and the Internet of Things. Many are ready to go in that they've proven they work and can add value:

- On the other hand, most companies and people on the business side have low levels of trust in their IT departments (see the box 'Trust between the business and IT'). It is hard to see how anything truly 'transformative' goes forward under these circumstances.
- Further, the data is not ready to go. At today's levels of data quality, AI is positively scary. Computer scientists and others have cited 'garbage in, garbage out', as a sort of tepid explanation, but transformation cannot succeed without high-quality data.

• On the one hand, existing systems, applications, and data structures 'work'. This says a lot, as there is so much to do, so many functions to automate, so much data to capture. Systems may be old, clunky, and require much handholding, but they get companies through the day. Further, basic storage, communications and processing technologies are already cheap and grow cheaper every day:

- On the other hand, most companies are saddled with massive technical debt, which makes it difficult to change anything. It seems as if everything new was simply bolted on, with little thought to an overall architecture.

Sorting out these contradictions will make it easier for companies to take greater advantage of their data (sorting out these contradictions is important for those hoping to take better advantage of information technology as well, but that is beyond the scope of this book).

TRUST BETWEEN THE BUSINESS AND IT

I was somewhat surprised when the lack of trust businesspeople had in their IT departments appeared on my radar screen. After all, tech companies such as Google, Facebook, Salesforce, Apple, IBM, SAP and plenty of others have been icons in the business world for some time now. People love their cell phones and the great apps that come with them. Finally, while people used to complain that 'Statistics was my least favourite course in college', STEM (science, technology, engineering and maths) courses are increasingly popular.

But as I asked around, businesspeople expressed their animosity in no uncertain terms. I heard comments such as, 'We really can't trust them to do anything important', 'Our systems don't talk', 'They are the least liked group in my company', and 'They cost too much'. Even throughout the pandemic, when IT teams scrambled to bring video conferencing, online ordering and other innovations to help save the day, such comments persisted. (One bit of good news: it does appear that many businesspeople enjoy working with individual IT team members, even if they dislike the department as a whole.)

For their parts, many tech people acknowledge there are issues between themselves and their business counterparts. They acknowledge that Tech departments sometimes fail to deliver but note that changing requirements are often the reason. Mostly they feel unappreciated. 'No one realizes how hard what we do is', pretty much sums up the frustration.

People and companies should pay more attention to trust quite generally. I've already cited lack of trust in data. And according to the ADP Research Institute, trust in colleagues, team leaders and senior leaders is at an all-time low.[1]

Data and information technology and different sorts of assets

Assigning the right people and departments to the most important tasks is job number 1 for senior managers, including data and information technologies. Commingling the two is a huge trap that continues to ensnare so many people and companies.

To see why, consider a 'movie' and the means by which you watch it. Not so long ago, the only way to watch a movie was to go to the theatre. Then along came TV and you could watch in your home, at times prescribed by networks. Then video cassettes, and you could watch any time you wanted. More recently, streaming technologies arrived, and now you can stream movies, on practically any device, and watch them any time and any place you want.

Streaming provides many advantages, but one thing it cannot do is change a bad movie into a good one! A bad movie is a bad movie (see the box 'Further on Information Technology and quality data').

FURTHER ON INFORMATION TECHNOLOGY AND QUALITY DATA

To be clear, new technologies may well help companies capture more and better data. A movie camera that captures images with greater resolution may make super-slow motion possible, surround sound speakers may make the action seem more immersive, and wide screen may provide a panoramic experience that a narrow screen does not. These are important advances and companies should seek to capture these advances.

The point remains however: slow motion, surround sound and a wider screen will not turn a bad movie into a good one. Nor can these technologies help the movie maker decide which scenes to shoot, the mix of good and bad traits in the lead actor, or how to lead in to the climactic scenes.

Now here is the key point – content and media are different sorts of assets. It takes a different skill set to make a movie than it does to create a network over which people can watch it. Managing the day-in, day-out work is different. Companies make money from them in different ways. Even as both are necessary if anyone is to view the movie, content and media are different sorts of assets.

In this analogy, the movie (the content) is the 'data' and the media by which you watch is the 'technology'. The technologies used to help create, store, process, access and help use the data are one sort of asset. But the actual data itself is created and used by the business and so must be managed by the business. Companies need both, of course, but data and information technology are different sorts of assets that require different skills to manage, use effectively and put to work. So you must manage data and the technologies used to store, move and process it separately.

Some may protest that data and technology are so entwined that you must manage them together. But that logic simply does not hold up – a company's employees use its company's financial assets to do their jobs, but that does not make the argument that the company should couple people and financial management. Further, people don't actually manage financial assets as much as data about them, using technology. But there is no confusion in specifying responsibilities for Tech, Finance and employees.

The biggest mistake of all lies in subordinating the data to the technology. Yet far too many companies, arguing that 'the data resides in the computer', make it. By this logic, people would report into Facilities Management! As Liz Kirscher, then Head of Data at Morningstar, the provider of mutual fund and other financial markets data, put it, 'We would no more have Tech run data than we would have Research run Tech!'[2]

The second biggest mistake lies in missing sources of value. It is easy to view Amazon, Facebook, Google and many others as technology companies. And indeed, they do deploy some rather impressive capabilities. But I think that view is incomplete, maybe even misleading. Consider Google, organizing the world's information. Similarly LinkedIn, whose mass of data about professionals enables it to identify 'connections' to help fuel peoples' career. And so on. Note that I am not saying technology isn't important – it certainly is. But companies should not let it obscure other sources of value.

It is clear enough that different sorts of assets require different management systems that recognize their special properties. For companies, step one is clear – you must be clear that the business has lead responsibility for data.[3] This responsibility extends to every single person, in their roles as data customers, data creators, decision-makers, protectors of company assets, and so forth. It includes metadata (e.g. data models, data dictionaries, data catalogues), definition and execution of privacy and security policy, and efforts to put data to work. If you've put leadership for data programmes inside IT, you must find them a better home. This is table stakes!

Freeing IT departments from responsibilities they should not have been assigned will remove a source of business unit dissatisfaction. It will allow IT to focus where it should be focussed on, which is developing a deeper understanding of the business, automating well-defined processes (more to follow), and sorting out which technologies are most likely to serve the company's long-term interests.

Information Technology departments are in tough spots

It seems no one can open their email these days without a barrage to the effect that digital transformation is taking over the world. Exciting stuff. If only it were true!

Of course we are used to hype. It may be the newest cosmetic, promising more youthful skin; a political pronouncement that the world will be saved, if only you vote for our candidate; or that some new product is a game changer. Within reason, we accept that those promoting a new product, idea or technology will describe it in its most favourable light. But it is another matter altogether when the product, idea or technology fails to deliver or distracts us from the real issues. In my view this is the case with digital transformation.

Digital transformation promises to exploit technological capabilities to radically transform customer interactions and business processes, improving both and disrupting entire industries. The aforementioned Amazon, Google and Uber testify to the potential. Today, there are plenty of potentially transformative technologies, from artificial intelligence, to blockchain, to data lakes, to 5G, to virtual reality ready to go.

Some claim that the pandemic accelerated digital transformation. By the end of 2020, we were where we might have been expected to be, absent the pandemic, in 2027, for example.[4] But other than technologies associated with Covid vaccines, I'm not impressed by the digital transformations of the last few years. It is true that video conferencing improved and that was helpful. And many stores and restaurants now provide the means to query their inventory databases and order online. I can find out whether the hardware store has the spray paint I need and order dinner on an app, drive there and have my order placed straight into my car. It replaces more manual efforts: calling, speaking to someone, going inside, etc. But these are hardly transformative.

Worse, too often the 'transformed processes' don't work all that well. Logistics and customer interactions are areas with extensive digitization. But supply chain woes are slowing economic recovery and may take years to sort out. And the jury is still out on digitized customer interactions. One 2021 summer evening my daughter-in-law remarked, 'We've used apps to order hundreds of meals since Covid. This is the first time I think they got everything right?!' It is a revelatory comment. People I talk to provide example after example – the home goods' website that said there was plenty of stock when there was none, the scheduling mishap, the online help desk that sends them in endless circles, never actually providing help, and so forth. Indeed, such indignities have caused some people to join the data generation.

Studies bear out the anecdotes, putting the failure rate in the 70–85 per cent range.[5,6,7] Too many 'transformations' simply don't work very well. Neil Gardner, advisor to Tech departments, summed it up this way, 'One big reason you're not impressed with digital transformation is that the vast majority fail.'[8]

These examples help explain why business departments don't trust their technology counterparts. They see the failures, the high costs and the lack of business understanding. Some businesspeople tell me that IT is the least respected of all corporate functions. I don't see how companies can digitally transform when they don't trust their IT departments.

Making matters worse still, the hype makes digital transformation seem easy – open up a process, pop in the new technology, and enjoy the benefits of improved customer satisfaction, lower cost and greater employee engagement in a few months. But digital transformation is really tough. It requires a rare combination of change management, process, data and technical talent.[9] Further, as Lacity and Van Hoek show in their study on blockchain, it can take years to assemble the coalition of players (e.g. regular people) needed, even when there is a clear, compelling business problem.[10]

Thus, those interested in pursuing digital transformation must first build trust and the only way to do that is to drastically reduce the basic errors noted above. But even that is not easy. As previously noted, all too often Technology Departments are asked to automate a poorly defined process, which leads to the sorts of errors that give it a bad reputation.

Exacerbating this is technical debt. Technical infrastructures have become confused messes and it is easy to see why. As one business department needs something new, IT works to provide it in the fast-est way possible, often adapting packaged software solutions from Salesforce, Oracle, SAP and a host of smaller best-of-breed providers. Each comes with its own data structures, so IT custom-crafts code to export, transform and load data from existing sources to feed these new data structures. All well and good.

But lacking a coherent architecture, customization becomes increas-ingly complex, adding more time and difficulty in meeting the next run-of-the-mill request, never mind meeting the rigours of true digital transformation. IT departments are in a tough spot. They are urged to 'get close to the business', but no one in the business is asking for a coherent infrastructure. That doesn't stop businesspeople from complaining that 'these systems don't talk', even as they were never designed to do so. Yet IT gets blamed and technical debt grows.

Compounding the situation, some IT departments have lost their ability to architect at the enterprise level. When I asked one CIO why it was so difficult to connect two mainstream production systems, he replied, 'Our architects can design stores, not the entire mall.'

IT is caught in a vicious cycle: demand for support or a new appli-cation rolls in, so IT concentrates on those requests, even as meeting them increases technical debt. This in turn makes it more difficult to satisfy business requests quickly, lessening business trust of IT. I'm sure many tech professionals feels like they are 'cycling the drain'.

Digital transformers, transform yourselves

What is to be done? To start I note that issues of trust, technical debt, and a backlog of needed technological upgrades have festered for a very long time. Resolving them will take a long time also. But some simple steps can help.

I find that nothing helps sort out broken relationships like the customer–supplier model, introduced in Chapter 7. It enables people, teams and departments to clarify roles, relationships and responsibilities. It helps them spot missing requirements and feedback channels, get out of the blame game, and find common ground.

So it is no surprise that, as a first step, IT and business departments must recognize roles for themselves as suppliers and customers. Most businesspeople readily accept that IT is a supplier, though a poor, overpriced one. But even a cursory glance will confirm that almost all business departments are even worse customers. The simple reality is that IT departments don't know what the business wants, largely because the business does not either. Those who want good technology simply must become better technology customers.

Step Two: stare down the hype. Too much misinformation, often from technology companies hawking their wares or consultants hawking their implementation services, poisons the relationships on both sides. As I've portrayed here, the reality is far more nuanced. To complete this work, conduct your own technology force field analysis (Tool A in the Toolkit). Use it to align all involved to the current reality.

The third step is to set reasonable expectations for IT. All the hype aside, it is difficult to sustain competitive advantage solely with IT. You can sustain advantage when you have something no one else has – a patented drug, unique knowledge surrounding chemical processes, or a licence arrangement that gives you exclusive access to a supply of a rare ingredient, a customer base, etc. Such things are 'proprietary assets', in that only one company has them and it can protect them over time. In Chapter 5, I urged regular companies to seek proprietary data as a means to create such an advantage.

Unless you are building your own, which few companies are, information technologies do not qualify as proprietary. They are freely for sale and, as noted, at increasingly lower prices. If you develop a clever AI algorithm and figure out how to use it first, you may well gain a measure of advantage. But it is difficult to sustain the advantage – the vendor who sold you the technology will look to license it further, key employees can take jobs with your competitors, and others follow the trail you blazed.

This is not to say that your business doesn't need the right mix of information technologies. It certainly does. Sorting out that mix and setting realistic expectations for your Technology department requires hard work by both business and Tech leaders.

I find the process summarized in Figure 8.1 helpful in doing so. It is based on ideas I first read about in John Roberts, modified somewhat with data in mind.[11]

Companies should work this process one step at a time, from left to right.[12] As Figure 8.1 makes clear, they can realistically expect their Technology departments to increase scale and decrease unit costs for well-defined, -controlled and -managed processes and data. Asking for much more is unlikely to work. One implication is that companies should not expect their Technology departments to clean up data messes or automate poorly defined processes.[13] Indeed, automating a bad process just means the company produces bad products, services and data faster. Nor should Technology departments be asked to better define business processes that they do not own. Conversely, Technology departments need to do a far better job pushing back when asked to do things they cannot do.

The second implication is that the business side must do a better job defining their work processes, getting them into a state where they can be automated and, if warranted, transformed.

The next step involves seeking some common ground around data. Even if Tech and the business agree on nothing else, all agree that data is essential and that it must be better managed. I've already noted that the business must take principal responsibility for data (e.g. content) and IT for technology (e.g. media). But where exactly is the line? Open-ended discussions on who is responsible for what when it comes to quality, security, metadata, common language, data architecture and storage can start to build trust and solve some important business problems.

FIGURE 8.1 Process for connecting strategy, organization, process and technology

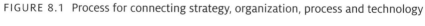

Finally, sooner or later, companies must take on technical debt, at least portions of it. To do so, as discussed in Chapter 7, they must first establish a common language. In turn, this will enable IT to simplify the data architecture, allowing the company to retire departmental systems, minimize work-arounds, and eliminate the need for custom interfaces. This reduces technical debt.

Perhaps the role model for using common language to reduce technical debt is Aera Energy LLC, an energy company based in Bakersfield, CA.[14] Formed from a merger, Aera found itself saddled with hundreds of non-integrated legacy systems and inconsistent information management practices. A major acquisition a year after the merger further compounded the problem. A few years later, Aera implemented an enterprise resource planning (ERP) system, which provided some integration and new functionality. But the company still had hundreds of legacy systems.

Aera leadership recognized the situation was growing increasingly untenable and that common language was needed to resolve the underlying issues. It took Aera only 53 core concepts to capture the essence of its business. These formed the heart of long-term data, application and technology architectures, allowing Aera to replace hundreds of systems over a several years and to add new capabilities.

Most important takeaways

- Great data programmes need great technology, but confusion about proper roles for data versus information technology, lack of trust and technical debt hold most companies back.

- Companies must separate the management of data and the management of information technologies.

- Rebuilding trust will take considerable time and good will on all sides.

- Companies should not expect the information technology departments to clean up data or automate poorly defined processes.

Instead they should narrow the expectations to increasing scale and decreasing unit costs.

- As trust grows, tech and business departments should work together to tackle technical debt.

Notes

1 M Buckingham. Becoming a more critical consumer of information, *Harvard Business Review*, 10 June 2021, hbr.org/2021/06/becoming-a-more-critical-consumer-of-information (archived at https://perma.cc/VUC2-S8DE)

2 TC Redman. Data's credibility problem, *Harvard Business Review*, December 2013, 84–88, hbr.org/2013/12/datas-credibility-problem (archived at https://perma.cc/99H5-2PTU)

3 TC Redman. Get responsibility for data out of IT, *Harvard Business Review* [blog] 22 October 2012, blogs.hbr.org/2012/10/get-responsiblity-for-data-out/ (archived at https://perma.cc/5UP4-QWMV)

4 See, for example, L LaBerge, C O'Toole, J Schneider and K Smaje. How Covid-19 has pushed companies over the technology tipping point – and transformed business forever, McKinsey & Company, 5 October 2020, www.mckinsey.com/business-functions/strategy-and-corporate-finance/our-insights/how-covid-19-has-pushed-companies-over-the-technology-tipping-point-and-transformed-business-forever# (archived at https://perma.cc/A2SQ-DPL9)

5 There is a rich literature here. For example (see also notes 6–7): A Alkhafaji. Why digital transformation fails, CMS Wire, 23 June 2021, www.cmswire.com/digital-experience/why-digital-transformation-fails/ (archived at https://perma.cc/WB5F-8HFV)

6 McKinsey & Co. Perspectives on transformation, www.mckinsey.com/capabilities/transformation/our-insights/perspectives-on-transformation (archived at https://perma.cc/D4LC-CK5J)

7 S Denning. Why digital transformations are failing, *Forbes*, 23 May 2021, www.forbes.com/sites/stevedenning/2021/05/23/why-digital-transformations-are-failing/?sh=5ab957627617 (archived at https://perma.cc/5DQR-XCGQ)

8 N Gardner, personal communication, 31 October 2022

9 TH Davenport and TC Redman. Digital transformation comes down to talent in 4 key areas, *Harvard Business Review*, 21 May 2020, hbr.org/2020/05/digital-transformation-comes-down-to-talent-in-4-key-areas (archived at https://perma.cc/6DFW-77CQ)

10 M Lacity and R Van Hoek. What we've learned so far about blockchain for business, *Sloan Management Review*, 1 February 2021, shop.sloanreview.mit.edu/store/what-weve-learned-so-far-about-blockchain-for-business (archived at https://perma.cc/KJA8-G9X7)

11 J Roberts (2020) *The Modern Firm: Organizational design for performance and growth,* Oxford University Press

12 TC Redman. The trust problem that slows digital transformation, *Sloan Management Review*, 26 July 2022, sloanreview.mit.edu/article/the-trust-problem-that-slows-digital-transformation/ (archived at https://perma.cc/L7TG-A7RM)

13 TC Redman and B Sweeney. Bridging the gap between IT and your business, *Harvard Business Review* [blog], 1 October 2013, blogs.hbr.org/2013/10/bridging-the-gap-between-it-and-your-business/ (archived at https://perma.cc/4LG5-GZG7)

14 D Hay, CL Yonke, TC Redman and J Zachman. Effective digital transformation depends on common language, *Harvard Business Review*, 14 December 2021, hbr.org/2021/12/effective-digital-transformation-relies-on-a-shared-language (archived at https://perma.cc/M5NN-482G)

9

Dream big, but change the culture one project at a time

NOTE: I anticipate that many senior leaders will skip directly to this chapter, so it contains several redundancies, to make it easier on those readers.

Senior management has stayed on the side-lines

As I discussed at length in Chapter 2, there have been plenty of great successes, 'points of light', where improved data quality and/or data science make a real mark. Still, the data is generally bad, adding enormous friction, and most data science projects fail. Even the big successes have not led to larger, enterprise-wide successes.

By and large, most senior executives have sat on the side-lines when it comes to data. They may have hired chief data officers, funded technological upgrades and signed off on privacy policies, but they have not fully engaged as they do on topics they feel are truly important. Neither have they (when it comes to data): provided the top-down leadership needed for true transformation; linked data and business priorities; provided the nurturing environment new ideas need to take root and flower; or addressed the organizational issues described herein (see the 'Time to get serious about data!' box).[1]

TIME TO GET SERIOUS ABOUT DATA!

New ideas come into companies through all sorts of channels: formal laboratories, vendor enticements, new employees, a middle manager seeking a fresh approach to a nagging problem. The vast majority of new ideas fail quickly. Some new ideas work well, and catch on within a particular niche.

But a few new ideas really catch on and things change quickly. The goal changes from incremental progress or a project-by-project mentality to rapid transformation. Companies muster an impressive breadth and depth of resources, they train and align people (e.g. naysayers are moved elsewhere), they constantly communicate new ways of working and values, and senior leaders drive the effort. I was very much impressed by AT&T's efforts to digitize its network early in my career. I heard about Amazon's Project D initiative to develop the Echo/Alexa smart speaker from my son and the urgency there feels similar. It appears that, when something is really urgent, they go overboard. People say 'failure is not an option' all the time in business. In these cases, it really is true! Senior leaders are in the middle of it all.

You can also tell when a company is not (yet) serious. It may say the right things and allow individuals and small teams to pursue projects, sometimes even big ones, but in truth it shows relatively little interest in those projects. Senior leaders don't attach themselves to these efforts or even help project teams deal with organizational issues, lest a failure derail their careers.

Many data programmes find themselves in the 'not (yet) serious' camp. For those new to data, this is understandable. But if you've been at it three years or more, this chapter is for you! It is probably time to make a decision: scale up or vector data programmes into niche roles.

At the same time, data programmes are crying out for leadership. Indeed, according to a University of Tennessee survey, only 10 per cent of companies have any sort of data strategy, never mind one that is fully coupled with business strategy.[2] Finally, as I've noted repeatedly, 'data is a team sport' and no team, in any environment, at either the project, business unit or project level, succeeds without effective leadership.

My goal in making these observations is not to be judgemental. It is to simply summarize the situation as best I can as a starting point for crafting a way forward.

Part of me sympathizes with senior leaders. For every data success there are at least two failures and the lingo – from 'the cloud' to data warehouses, to data lakes, to data-driven cultures – is a confused mess. Most importantly, I've pointed out that any individual, team leader or manager can make important contributions to their team's success using data with no help whatsoever from senior leaders.

But their efforts will only go so far. Today's organizations are especially unfit for data in that they make it far too difficult for people to follow the 'data is a team sport' mantra at scale. I described many of the specific issues and the directions for solution in Chapters 7 and 8. Unfortunately, individuals, team leaders and managers cannot resolve the issues on their own. This requires top-down leadership, the direct, personal involvement of a company's most senior executives.

So, what, exactly, should senior leaders do? To answer, this chapter proposes two major responsibilities:

- building a better organization for data and
- putting data to work

These are 'non-delegatable' in the sense that success or failure in both rests on their shoulders. To be more specific, a company's senior leaders must:

A. Build a better organization for data:

   i. Embrace a culture that values data, gets everyone involved and promotes teamwork. After all, as much as anything else, it is data that binds the company together.

   ii. Make several key hires/appointments, including the head(s) of data, the head of the data science bridge, the head of common language, and putting them in the right spots. Put someone who understand data on your Board.

   iii. Help these hires/appointees build the rest of the organization, starting with a network of embedded data managers and continuing until everyone understands how they can, and must, contribute.

B. Put data to work:

    i. Attack data quality to improve current performance, to provide the investment dollars to fund the rest of the data programme, and because high-quality data is a prerequisite for putting data to work.

    ii. Connect the data programme and business priorities.

The remainder of the chapter takes up each in turn.

Building a better organization for data

I don't know of a company that has thought deeply enough about the features of the data culture it would like to create. Some don't even try, openly admitting that they view data as the 'exhaust' of their real work. Others confuse data and technology. Still others may blithely proclaim that 'our data is an asset', blissfully ignoring two hard truths. First, most data is never used – it is hard to see how it qualifies as assets, even if it meets a strict accountant's definition. Second, so much data that does get used is bad – it is hard to see how it qualifies as anything other than a liability. Some data may indeed qualify as assets, but that blanket statement makes it harder to suss out which! Finally, some encourage their charges to 'make data-driven decisions', as if they are using a Ouija board today. None of this is helpful.

That said, a company's data culture does matter. As I've previously explained, as much as anything else, data binds the company together, or pushes it apart. If people acknowledge and try to meet the needs of data customers in other teams, people and the company come together. If they do not do so, people retreat further into their silos, pushing the company apart.

Senior leaders should ask themselves four questions regarding their company's data futures, as depicted in Figure 9.1:

1 Do we see data as empowering the many (per my 'get everyone involved' mantra), the province of a few, perhaps a small cadre of professionals (as is usually the case today), or something in between?

2 Do we see that data should be broadly shared and that diverse, cross-departmental teams should use data to create new opportunities (per my 'data is a team sport' mantra), that each team should tend to its own data needs (as is the de facto approach today), or something in the middle?

3 Do we see data, some of it anyway, as a new and sustaining source of new value (if managed properly, data can be an asset), not worthy of special attention (it helps people do their work, just like a well-lit environment helps them), or something in between?

4 Do we see high-quality (trusted, accurate, relevant, etc) data as table stakes, as not worth added effort, or somewhere in between?

When posed this way, most articulate their preferences closer to the first options, on the right of Figure 9.1, than to the second ones, on the left. They may see their preferences as for the distant future, but that is fine – changing the culture is a long-term proposition. I've been privileged to see it happen, at least partially, with several of my clients. In those cases, actions have spoken louder than words. They simply started to attack quality, manage data more professionally, and use a bit more of it to drive their decisions, and a new normal permeated the culture.

Confronted with these realities, senior leaders should think through the culture they'd like to create, then behave as though it were in

FIGURE 9.1   Where does data fit in you company's future?

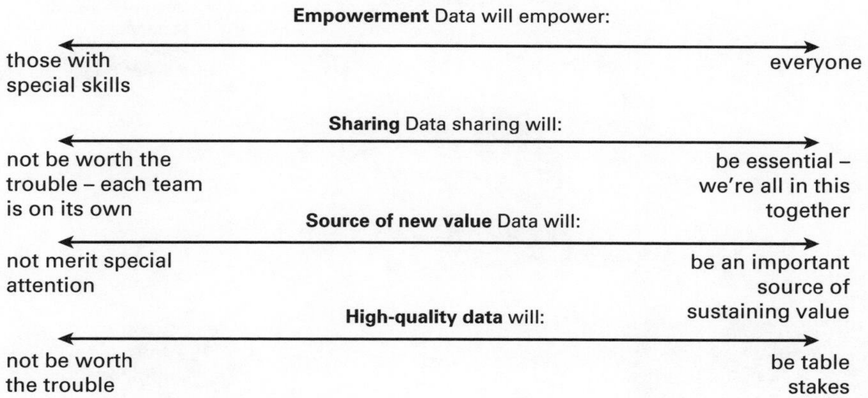

Empowerment Data will empower:

those with special skills ←—————————————————————————→ everyone

Sharing Data sharing will:

not be worth the trouble – each team is on its own ←—————————————————————————→ be essential – we're all in this together

Source of new value Data will:

not merit special attention ←—————————————————————————→ be an important source of sustaining value

High-quality data will:

not be worth the trouble ←—————————————————————————→ be table stakes place. Recognize that you are a data creator and a data customer, just like everyone else, take up your responsibilities as such, and become a role model for your subordinates and peers. Then build a better organization for data.

Selecting options towards the right of the figure means getting everyone to contribute to data quality efforts, work on small data projects, learn to use more data to make better decisions, and contribute to larger programmes to put data to work. It calls for a highly federated organization for data, as I've argued for throughout and as proposed in Figure 9.2 (first presented in Chapter 3).

But even as responsibility for data is pushed out, I am not calling for anarchy. Responsibilities must be clarified in policy and people trained to do what is expected. So too I've argued for 'fat organizational pipes' that connect people, make it easier to share data, to get on the same page, and to work together.

Building such an organization is senior management's most important job. This means making four key hires/appointments and getting them in the right spots. Let's start with the **Head of Data** (HoD).

Companies are using a variety of titles for this role: Chief Data Officer and Chief Analytics Officer appear to be among the most

FIGURE 9.2 Components of a better organization for data: four key appointments

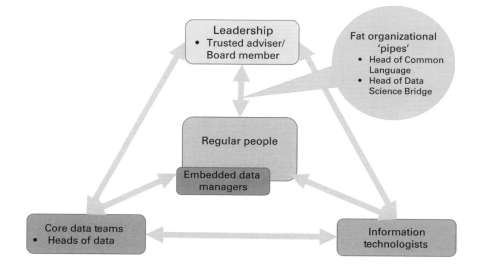

common. These titles reflect different emphases: CDOs on getting the basics right and CAOs on using advanced analytics to improve the business. Most companies need both roles and many companies combine the roles into a single CDAO.

Look for people like Jeff MacMillan, Wealth Management, Morgan Stanley and Mai AlOwaish at Gulf Bank. Jeff began his data career decades ago; this is Mai's first data role. They share three common traits: their passion for data, superb communications skills, and the ability to work with others. I don't see this third trait mentioned nearly enough, but it is essential, because to be effective, CDOs must engage with others in the company. Mai has developed a great relationship with Human Resources, which views her as leading changes that are essential to the entire bank.

Now, to whom should HoDs report? Jeff reports to Andy Saperstein, who runs the Wealth Management Business; Mai to Raghu Menon, Deputy CEO, both excellent choices. As discussed in Chapter 8, the worst choice is having your HoDs report to your Chief Information (Technology) Officer. Data and technology are different kinds of assets and co-mingling their management has slowed progress on both. If your CDO reports into IT today, look for a better home.

THE HOD'S MOST IMPORTANT JOB

I advise HoDs (or the most senior data person if no one holds that title) that their number one job is to 'train up'. For there is no way that senior executives, no matter how analytical their bent, can understand enough about data to provide the business leadership needed. No one is better positioned to help them understand the issues and opportunities than HoDs (and possibly a Board member).

The HoD's most important task is to 'train up' (see the 'A note on training' box). Next on the list, HoDs must recruit a large network of *embedded data managers* from every department/team across the company (as previously noted, about one person per 40, in part-time roles) who in turn help get everyone involved. As a practical matter, senior leadership must help recruit these people, who will continue to report into their business departments, while at the same time functioning as members of the extended data team. Finally, HoDs must build centres of excellence, including data quality, data science, privacy, security, etc, in areas that advance the company's business strategies.

Two other appointees are especially important: the Head of Common Language and the Head of the Data Science Bridge. The notion of common language sounds so maddeningly arcane and technical that it is hard to imagine any senior leader who would want to get involved. But that instinct is wrong for three reasons:

1 Senior management bears full responsibility for the ways departments interact and common language is essential if they are to do so effectively.

2 The costs of not having common language are high.

3 Spotting opportunities to develop common language and put it in place requires experience and judgement.

Thus, senior leaders need to name a very senior manager, with the authority, gravitas, level and judgement to: call out the need for common language; develop, weigh, and if appropriate, sell the business case; set direction; provide resources; align others; and enlist them to contribute. I call this person the **Head of Common Language (HoCL)**. They can be the HoD, the head of strategy, perhaps even the head of human resources. Most of the time, this is a part-time role, but one that requires great judgement. For developing common language is difficult, only justified by extremely important issues. Once a compelling opportunity is identified, it becomes a full-time role, with plenty of overtime!

Similarly, while a data science centre of excellence aims to disrupt business processes, the managers of those processes aim to maintain stability – goals that are fundamentally at odds. Addressing this structural barrier means you have to build a data science 'bridge' connecting the two. The person heading it up is called the **Head of the Data Science Bridge (HoDSB)**. Based on work with co-authors Roger Hoerl and Diego Kuonen, and early experiences, this person should report as high up the management chain as possible.

Finally, you need someone who understands data to push you to go further and faster than you might otherwise be inclined, serve as a sounding board as you evaluate options, and help you anticipate and deal with resistance. The ideal candidate has both an expansive vision and scars on their back from hard-fought battles in advancing a data agenda. The two possible routes involve finding a trusted advisor or putting someone on the Board. (NOTE: Full transparency, I sometimes serve in this capacity.)

A NOTE ON TRAINING

Training people is going to take time and cost money. Some may complain that these will be excessive. I think not, especially when compared to the (unknown) costs of what you can't do if people aren't facile with data. Embedded data managers need about two total days of training. At Gulf Bank, embedded data managers attend five hands-on workshops over six months. The sessions for regular people are delivered by HR. These sessions feature core concepts that are the same for everyone plus customized examples, i.e. branches see different examples than regulatory reporting. I bring this up because managers reluctant to participate will cite 'lack of budget' as excuses for non-participation. Senior leadership may decide to fund the training effort to obviate this excuse.

Putting data to work

Attack poor data quality

As it turns out, almost everyone shares a common experience – wasting valuable time correcting errors, dealing with disparate systems, and checking up on numbers that just don't look right. Finance teams tell me they spend three-quarters of their time reconciling reports, decision-makers don't believe the numbers and instruct their staff to validate them, and Sales teams a couple of hours each day cleaning up leads from Marketing. Bad data is an equal opportunity peril![3]

The total costs are enormous – think 20 per cent of revenue.[4] Nor does all this clean-up go well, as most people readily admit they don't trust the data. Further bad data pushes people apart, exactly as I've railed against. These costs are not captured in accounting systems, rather, they are hidden away in day-in, day-out work.

The secret to wasting less time and money involves changing everyone's approach – from the current 'buyer/user beware' mentality where everyone is left on their own to deal with bad data, to creating data correctly the first time. This works because finding and eliminating a single root cause can prevent thousands of future errors – and the need to correct them downstream. When people step into their roles as data customers and data creators, improvements come quickly. And the attendant savings, up to three-quarters of the costs cited above, are enormous.

Thus senior leaders should declare all-out war on bad data. They should task the HoD with coordinating the effort and tap into the network of embedded data managers. Doing so is important in its own right: better data removes a source of frustration and makes all processes work more smoothly. Finally, they can use the savings as investment dollars for the rest of the data agenda.

Connect data and business priorities

In almost every company I've worked with, I find a big disconnect between those working on data and the business priorities of senior leadership. Too many data people pursue 'data for data's sake' and too many senior executives don't see how data and data science can advance the business. Is it any wonder that data programmes fail!

Making the needed connections brings three inputs together, as depicted in Figure 9.3: data, business priorities and data 'value modes'. At the centre of the figure are values modes, ways data can improve business performance (see the 'Data value modes' box).[5] We find that both business and data leaders understand these value modes and can use them as a lingua franca to align their respective programmes. In particular, they facilitate disciplined thinking, narrow the focus, and drive the right conversations.

There is no magic here. In Figure 9.3, to align the data programme to overall business strategy, work back and forth via the value modes between the data programme and the business programme, taking

FIGURE 9.3 Connecting data with business strategy

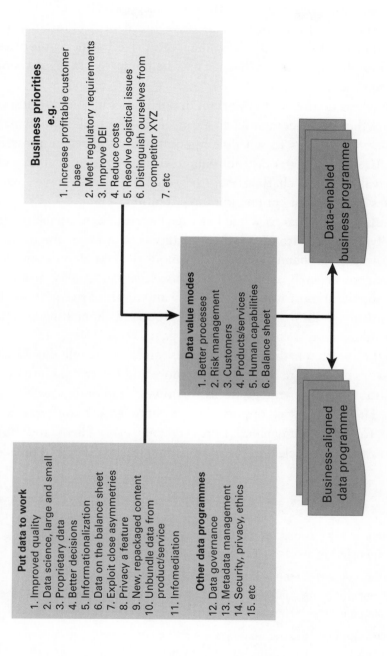

Put data to work

1. Improved quality
2. Data science, large and small
3. Proprietary data
4. Better decisions
5. Informationalization
6. Data on the balance sheet
7. Exploit close asymmetries
8. Privacy a feature
9. New, repackaged content
10. Unbundle data from product/service
11. Infomediation

Other data programmes

12. Data governance
13. Metadata management
14. Security, privacy, ethics
15. etc

Business priorities e.g.

1. Increase profitable customer base
2. Meet regulatory requirements
3. Improve DEI
4. Reduce costs
5. Resolve logistical issues
6. Distinguish ourselves from competitor XYZ
7. etc

Data value modes

1. Better processes
2. Risk management
3. Customers
4. Products/services
5. Human capabilities
6. Balance sheet

Data-enabled business programme

Business-aligned data programme

the new possibilities that data offers into account. (NOTE: While one may expect business priorities to drive the data programme, it is important to also consider how data can drive business priorities.) For example, artificial intelligence may help improve many decision-making processes.

But where do the most important opportunities lie and how important are they to the company? In a cancer centre, chatbots may make it easier for patients to schedule appointments and renew prescriptions. Useful, but better decisions about courses of treatment are even more valuable. So chatbots may be rated as 'nice to have', while courses of treatment command more attention.

Similarly with quality. While I've urged executives to attack quality broadly, there are also areas where quality is of strategic importance. For example, companies aiming to be among the best at understanding their customers may require world-class levels of quality. Similarly, companies that must watch every nickel and dime may require world-class quality so they can improve their processes, eliminating as much of the added costs associated with bad data as possible.

As they work together, senior business and data people should seek new ways to put data to work, drive more and better data into every important business strategy, decision, process, and onto your balance sheet. They should seek opportunities to both 'go big' and 'go small'. Small to make incremental improvements everywhere and build organizational muscle and big to take on a few really big challenges.

DATA VALUE MODES

1 **Improving business processes:** Doing the basic operational, reporting and managerial work in better ways and/or at lower cost.

2 **Improving risk management:** Leveraging better data about competitors, meeting regulator expectations, and so forth, to protect the company against threats.

3 **Developing a deeper understanding of customers:** Growing deeper richer relationships with customers to increase stickiness and/or better tailor products and services to meet their needs.

4 **Developing new and/or improved products and services:** Building data into products or services to make them more valuable. Using proprietary data to provide offerings the competitors can't match.

5 **Improving human capabilities:** Helping people grow in their jobs, in turn making them happier and more productive. Better decision-making is one important result.

6 **Improving the balance sheet:** Sorting out how to treat data as assets in the sense that they are on the balance sheet (presumably improving it).

They should give the 'human capabilities' value mode, the major theme of this book, special consideration. Since few are doing so now, this may be the easiest way to distinguish yourself from others and create a source of advantage in tight labour markets.

Senior leaders should also give special consideration to proprietary data and the 'improved products and services' value mode. Companies don't compete based on the ways in which they are similar to others, but on the ways in which they differ from the crowd. Importantly, each company's data is uniquely its own, a potentially huge, untapped source of new value, and exploiting data you have and others don't may present special opportunities.

Most important takeaways

- Eventually, all change is top-down, but by and large senior leaders have not chosen to engage in data programmes. The impact is debilitating.

- Senior leaders bear non-delegatable responsibilities for the data programme in two main areas: building a better organization for data, including clarifying the data culture they would like to create; and connecting business and data priorities.

Notes

1 TC Redman and TH Davenport. Getting serious about data and data science, *MIT Sloan Management Review*, 28 September 2020, sloanreview.mit.edu/article/getting-serious-about-data-and-data-science/ (archived at https://perma.cc/W6EZ-9CRR)

2 R Bradley and M Long. Time to sync your digital, analytics, and data strategies, Working paper, October 2021

3 T Nagle, T Redman and D Sammon. Only 3% of companies data meets basic quality standards, *Harvard Business Review*, September 2017, hbr.org/2017/09/only-3-of-companies-data-meets-basic-quality-standards (archived at https://perma.cc/S32U-CG8N)

4 TC Redman. Seizing opportunity in data quality, *MIT Sloan Management Review*, 27 November 2017

5 John Ladley is responsible for the value mode concept. See: J Ladley and TC Redman. Use data to accelerate your business strategy, *Harvard Business Review*, 3 March 2020, hbr.org/2020/03/use-data-to-accelerate-your-business-strategy (archived at https://perma.cc/5LBE-WMVR)

10

The data teams companies need now

Clear management responsibility

Throughout this book, I've tried to be extremely clear regarding who is responsible for what regarding data. I've called out and clarified responsibilities for regular people, tech teams, leaders, data supply chain managers, common language leaders and the head of the data science bridge. Most will find these responsibilities new and unfamiliar. People need a lot of direction, training, support and encouragement to succeed. The day-in, day-out work of providing that help falls to data teams. This chapter addresses the data teams companies need now: what they do, where they fit, how existing data teams must grow and change.

This requires some fresh thinking. So this chapter starts by exploring five factors that should guide the design of data teams, including their principal responsibilities and where they should fit. The analysis digs into the traits of the people needed to lead them. Next, we'll dig into three key directions that are just beginning to wind their ways into practice on the data teams companies need now. Finally, we'll conclude with a discussion of Gulf Bank's first year putting these ideas into practice.

Five factors guiding the design of data teams

1. Get the work done

In 'Are you asking too much of your chief data officer?', Davenport and Bean cite seven roles of CDOs.[1] Their principal concern is that chief data officers are held to unreasonable expectations, possibly contributing to the high failure rate associated with the position. At the same time, they acknowledge that someone must do all the work:

1 **Chief Data and/or Analytics Officer**: oversight of data management, data science and analytics

2 **Data Entrepreneur**: monetizing data

3 **Data Developer**: development of key applications and/or infrastructure capabilities (e.g. data warehouses, lakes)

4 **Data Defender**: keep data safe from breaches, keeping data safe from bad guys, dealing with regulators

5 **Data Architect**: ensuring that key data is organized, aggregated, cleansed and ready for use

6 **Data Governor**: ensure proper oversight of data

7 **Data Ethicist**: set and execute policies that dictate how data is collected, kept safe, shared and controlled

Importantly, Bean and Davenport do not include 'lead the quality programme' in their list. This reflects the fact that most companies have not yet taken up this work, even as it is essential to success elsewhere. I propose to add it as an 8th 'must have':

8 **Data Quality Leaders**: lead efforts to manage and improve data quality

2. Get everyone involved

Much of this book has urged regular people to see opportunity for themselves in data and carve out better jobs for themselves. I hope companies will encourage them to do so. But whether they do so or not, this book has pointed out that data programmes cannot succeed without them. In particular, regular people must assume key roles, as data customers and creators, as small data scientists, as guardians of the company's data assets, as contributors to larger data initiatives and as better decision-makers. Bringing them up to speed is a large essential, and the 9th task for data teams:

9 Data Trainers: train regular people for their roles and responsibilities for data going forward and help them succeed in those roles

At the risk of being repetitive, managers and senior leaders are regular people also. They need even more training and support than everyone else. So 'training up the organization chart' is especially important. (As previously noted, in my view this is one of the most important jobs of the most senior person with 'data' in their title.)

In a slightly different vein, most companies readily accept that everyone must follow privacy policy, become better decision-makers, and help others where needed. But, as discussed in Chapter 7, the notion that regular people are both data customers and data creators is another matter altogether. It is observably true, and obvious once pointed out. It is also transformational because it changes expectations and relationships. It assigns people responsibilities they never had before. To a lesser extent, the idea that everyone is a small data scientist is also transformational. Some groups, presumably a data team, must lead and guide this transformation. Thus, a 10th task for data teams:

10 Data Transformers: lead change

3. Data is a team sport

I've repeatedly emphasized that working effectively with data requires exceptional degrees of cooperation, far more than most companies exhibit today. First, data creators and customers must work together to improve quality; increasingly large numbers of people must work together on increasingly large data projects; fairly large groups must work together to establish common language, and cooperate across complex supply chains. People must bridge silos, establish common language, and work together even when the tensions between them are designed in. This too requires transformation, reinforcing the point above.

Secondly, it bears mention that good data programmes are messy, with people and teams flying off in a thousand different directions. The idea of strong, top-down control is antithetical to turning regular people loose as they learn and grow accustomed to their new roles. Someone has to pull everything together, to steer things in rough directions, to evaluate progress, and most importantly of all, to ensure a certain level of coordination. I might be tempted to say 'orchestrate' the action, as if a bunch of unskilled musicians were to somehow come together as one and play a great symphony. I hope that as individual players gain skill and management becomes more facile with data, companies can indeed 'orchestrate' their data programmes. For now, let's aim for coordination:

11 Data Programme Coordinators: assemble the right groups of people, encourage them to work together, and help them do so

4. Business priorities

The last thing that those promoting a data agenda should do is set up their programmes without fully attaching those programmes to business priorities. Most pertinently, they should craft data teams and locate them to increase the chances that they will advance these priorities. There is a bit of a 'chicken and egg' problem here – it is hard to set priorities until business teams know what data can do for them and it is hard for them to see what data can do until data teams are in place to demonstrate. Everyone involved must do their best in light of this issue.

5. The E- and F-factors

Although I don't know how to quantify it, I find that some data efforts move way further and faster than others. One can check the boxes – leadership, yes; clear objectives, yes; people know what they're supposed to do, yes; right people involved, yes. Still, some projects proceed more quickly, with greater confidence, and with hurdles more easily surmounted. Some programmes have greater reach and produce broader, deeper, more long-lasting results.

And while my analysis is anecdotal, I chalk these successes up to *empowerment* and *fun*, the E- and F-factors. Quite simply, people feel empowered. They want to keep their bosses informed, but they don't want to go running back for permission on every little thing. They lean in to engage people, make decisions, to go the extra mile. Certainly, not one of them wants to make mistakes, but people know their data project is entering uncharted territory and mistakes are inevitable. They feel empowered to admit mistakes and learn from them.

Similarly, fun. It's fun to take control of your work life, to learn new things, to make things better. You can almost always tell if a data programme or project is going well, because people are having a good time. Not every day of course. There are plenty of setbacks. But overall, the work is pleasurable.

It leads me to add a 12th and final design criterion – empowering people and making the work fun:

12 Data Cheerleaders: help people empower themselves and make work fun

Clearly there are many powerful criteria to guide the composition, placement and leadership of data teams. They lead to some different ways to think about staff, and the position of data teams. We'll not discuss much how they do their work, as that could fill volumes.

Towards more effective data teams

As the new kids on the block, data science, strategy, governance and protection teams have had to establish themselves. Quite naturally, they have selected problems they could work on by themselves. Quality teams have focussed on data clean-up, data science teams on areas where there is lots of data, and privacy teams on developing the policies needed to meet the General Data Protection and other regulations. While understandable, this internal focus excludes regular people, counter to many of the factors outlined above.

Therefore, data teams must reorient their work. They must:

- engage regular people every day
- develop a feel for their problems and opportunities
- embrace their hopes and fears surrounding data
- focus less on big data and more on equipping people with the tools they need to formulate and solve their own problems

In short, data teams must seek joy, not in a clever model, but in business results and in empowering those they serve.

This point is easiest to see with data quality. A natural first step is to implement a data quality tool that will help clean up data faster. It can make an immediate impact and there is some logic to the approach – the company will spend less time cleaning up data. But it is a bad idea, as it does not address root causes of errors, and clean-up will never end. Instead, companies should make clear that business departments are responsible for their own data quality and that they must find and eliminate root causes of errors. The only way to do that is through regular people.

For data quality teams, this means changing their role from doing the work to helping regular people rid themselves of the 'deal with mundane data issues' portions of their jobs.

> The resonant theme for data teams is a shift from an 'inside-out' to an 'outside-in' perspective. It should lead to a redeployment of personnel: towards strategic problems, towards small data, towards rooting out quality issues, and towards empowerment. It means more training, day-in, day-out assistance and coaching; less technical work; far greater impact. Exciting for companies. Exciting and scary for data professionals.

Figure 10.1 presents three key features of the extended data teams companies need now. First, small powerful teams of *data professionals* [shaded grey], each with the expertise to guide efforts in specified areas such as data quality or data science. Still, the number of data

FIGURE 10.1 Business departments and the extended data team

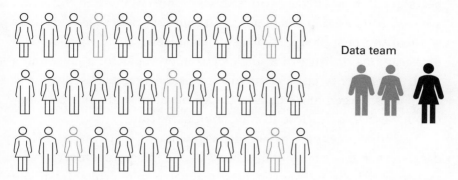

professionals (e.g. people with data in their titles) is small relative to the number of regular people.

The second feature, a network of *embedded data managers* [outlined in grey], fills the gap. Embedded data managers may also be called ambassadors (as at Gulf Bank), responsible parties (as at Chevron), provocateurs (as described in Chapter 4), lovers of data, local champions, role models, or even citizen data scientists. They may have no title whatsoever, simply be more quantitative, more interested in improving their team's performance, or more interested in making a name for themselves and willing to help others and push data in their work teams.

The third feature is *team leaders* [in black] with the courage to get their teams out there.

The extended data team therefore consists of data team members, leaders and embedded data managers, such that all regular people are able to connect with an extended data team member, and are expected to contribute to the data programme.

The following subsections discuss each in turn. I will not discuss 'how' each data team does its work. That would take volumes.

Small, powerful, close-to-the-action core teams

The sheer number and magnitude of the five factors makes clear that there is much to do, and in many diverse areas. Companies will need lots of teams, with a variety of specialties. Exactly what they need depends on their business priorities. With the exception of some necessary staff work, data teams should report as close to the action as possible. I find that small, powerful teams work best, even as there is a real shortage of skilled professionals. Here, 'small' is relative. A data team may consist of a single person, even part of a person in a small company. A large company requires larger teams. In bigger companies, larger, more data-intensive business units and divisions may have their own close-to-the-action data teams.

First, companies need a data management team(s) to organize their data, store it, move it around, process it, and integrate it together just as before. This data management team can and probably should report into IT or a Chief Data Officer.

Companies also need security teams to keep the bad guys from stealing their data and privacy teams to make sure they themselves don't use the data inappropriately. In many countries, security and privacy concerns mandate that companies name a Protection Officer, even as privacy and security are two different things. Given their potential exposure, many Protection Officers report into Legal departments which, from my perspective, represents a missed opportunity. As noted in Chapter 6, I see privacy and privacy policy as a feature and a potential source of advantage. It might be better if Protection Officers and privacy teams reported into Marketing or Product Development.

Next, almost all companies need a team(s) with deep expertise and experience in data quality. Data quality teams must do a certain amount of staff work to manage the overall programme. In this capacity, they must import and adapt the approaches, methods and tools to be used; maintain an overall scorecard; keep senior leaders abreast of progress; and continually sell the effort. Still, the majority of its time should be spent with embedded data managers and regular people, training them to become better data creators and data customers and helping them do the work. Those managing data supply chains are most likely regular people and they often need special assistance from quality professionals. So too is the executive assigned to monitor the need for common language. A very senior quality professional should be assigned to this effort.

Much depends on getting data quality teams right. As I've argued throughout, it is more difficult to do anything when the data is bad.

Now consider data science, where the range of potential for data science teams is enormous. On one end of the spectrum, many companies are exploring big data, advanced analytics and artificial intelligence. Justifiably so, as these techniques and technologies offer opportunities to attack problems that cannot be simply solved with more traditional methods, and they offer opportunities to take costs out of repetitive decision processes. But big data, advanced analytics and AI projects and programmes are devilishly difficult to pull off. It is easy to get distracted, data quality can be a real issue, and implementation presents real challenges. Companies pursuing them need some sort of 'AI centre of excellence' or 'data science lab' largely isolated from day-in, day-out issues. They also need a Data Science Bridge, as described in Chapter 7.

This excitement aside, most companies should spend most of their data science effort on the other end of the size/sophistication spectrum, focussing on small data. As noted, they are loaded with problems that can be solved with small teams, small amounts of data, in a short amount of time, and with high probability of success. Many know this. I sometimes ask companies, 'Which would you rather have: a newly minted PhD data scientist or 20 people who can help regular people conduct basic analyses in their current jobs?' Almost all opt for the latter. Small data teams work much like their data quality counterparts (some companies combine the two). There is a certain amount of staff work, but much more teaching and assistance.

In contrast to data science centres of excellence, which must be isolated from the din of day-in, day-out work, small data science teams are designed to embrace that din. As such they should be aligned as close to the action as possible.

There are also many 'mid-range' problems. For example, a sophisticated model may require considerable maintenance by professional data scientists, a one-time problem may motivate an ad hoc project team from across the company, or a problem may be of strategic importance. Teams working such problems, at either the project or programme level, must balance these two trade-offs: get too close and they get lost in the day-to-day; stay too far apart and they don't engage the full range of people needed to succeed.[2,3]

Lastly, the company's most senior data person bears two special responsibilities:

- educating senior management on the potential and challenges in data and their roles and
- ensuring that the overall data programme addresses the company's most important issues and opportunities

I use the term 'governance' for this oversight role (NOTE: Over the past 10 years or so, the term 'governance' has acquired a sprawl of meanings. This is unfortunate. Here, I only use data governance to mean oversight.)

Embedded data managers, even closer to regular people

I've noted that data teams are small compared to the size of the rest of the company and that it is ridiculous to think that they (data teams) can connect with enough regular people to make a real difference. Thus embedded data managers fill an important gap. These people report into their business groups and so are close enough to help regular people day in, day out.

As a starting estimate, each department should have about one part-time embedded data manager per 40 people, though I expect considerable variation around that ratio – teams that use more data may well require more. And to be clear, while they have a dotted line relationship with data teams, their solid line reporting relationships are into their business departments. First and foremost, these are businesspeople, responsible to their departments and their goals.

Their responsibilities include:

- Leading data and data quality efforts within their teams. This means assisting regular people in taking on their roles as data customers and data creators and completing small data projects, as two important examples.
- Assisting regular people in understanding their roles in larger data science projects.

- Helping other embedded data managers make needed connections. For example, a data customer may need help finding a data creator three departments upstream. Or an embedded data manager may represent their departments on data supply chain management teams.

- Serving as the 'tip of the spear' in advancing the notion that a company's data, as much as anything else, binds the company together. Everyone must be involved AND they must work with others.

- Making sure that everyone understands privacy and security policy and assist if there are any questions in implementation.

- Representing their departments in efforts to establish, promulgate and maintain common language.

Leaders with gravitas

Over the years I've advised many great leaders of data teams and seen even more in action. I've also seen plenty fail. Some blundered into a bad situation, others overestimated what they could achieve, and some made the mistake of taking an inside-out focus. They may have come up with some great stuff, but failed to launch.

Perhaps no management topic has received as much study as leadership and all of it applies to data leaders. Here, I'll simply offer a few additional observations.

First, great data leaders have a simpler, better idea that they communicate clearly and often. Consider attacking the root causes of data errors. It is objectively simpler and more effective than making errors in one part of the company and cleaning them up in another. It is simply a better idea, even if does mean that regular people must step up in their roles as data customers and data creators.

That's the 'better mousetrap' part of the trait. The other part, communicating it clearly and often, is just as important. Leaders have a knack for getting people to see that better way without feeling attacked for not seeing it before.

The great data leaders are incredibly level-headed. They know how difficult what they hope to achieve is, they are fully aware of the strengths and limitations of their teams and of themselves. Great data leaders are careful not to overextend themselves and their teams, preferring to move from one success to the next. Though I don't think I've ever heard one say, 'data is a team sport', they seem to intuitively grasp the concept. Thus, they build support, engaging business large numbers of people and taking time to understand their perspectives. They don't hesitate to ask for help, both from peers and superiors. And while they bear outsize responsibility for their team's successes, they are gracious in sharing credit.

Great data team leaders are persistent, sometimes even stubborn. Even the most successful data programmes experience loads of failures. Great data leaders keep their longer-term objectives in mind, seeing failure as an opportunity to learn more than anything else.

Finally, they are relentless, even incurable optimists. Their optimism makes them fun to be around and helps attract people with can-do attitudes to their team and to their cause.

CASE STUDY
The first year for the Gulf Bank data team

The first year of the data programme at Gulf Bank, the Kuwait City-based consumer and commercial bank, illustrates what companies should expect of data teams, and what data teams should expect of themselves if they adapt the guidance provided here to their circumstances. (NOTE: Full disclosure – I advised Gulf Bank during this year.) Gulf Bank has 2,000 employees and operates about 50 branches across the country.

This story kicks off with the hiring of its first Chief Data Officer, Mai AlOwaish. Her experiences in banking, e-commerce and data consulting all came together for this newly added role, and in her words, 'was an exciting challenge'.

AlOwaish reported into Raghunandan Menon, Deputy CEO, a seasoned banking veteran, who was well aware of the high failure rate of data programmes. His number one instruction was, 'First get the basics right.' This advice was crucial. Too many data programmes are saddled with the demand that they show 'quick wins'. While the sentiment is understandable, it is also often unachievable – real wins are hard and too often lead to unrealistic expectations.

AlOwaish decided that data quality was fundamental and put it on the top of her list. Doing so was not at all obvious. Gulf Bank was pursuing an upgrade to its core systems – working on the associated data issues (e.g. common language) was a strong competitor. But she decided to gain some experience and credibility first. So, she alerted senior management of her concerns and her decision. Getting no pushback, she pressed on with quality.

Her next steps were to build the necessary organizational capabilities. This meant building her own small team and building the network of embedded data managers, whom she called 'ambassadors'. Mai made a few key internal hires, including Sabeeka AlRashed, whose previous role was in Gulf Bank's Treasury Department. She immediately recognized that the notions of 'data customer' and 'data creator' would prove transformative. AlRashed led work to create the data quality curriculum, which would be aimed first at ambassadors, and then for everyone in the bank as part of AlOwaish's data literacy initiative. Fouzan AlSumait, a data analyst from the Call Centre who had a passion for data, took charge of training the data ambassadors as part of the transformation. They decided the best approach would be to provide in-person, interactive training for small groups, so the ambassadors could better absorb what was in store for them. And Aws AlAnsari, whom AlOwaish hired from outside, led work to help ambassadors baseline data quality.

Along the way, AlOwaish and AlSumait added small data to their portfolio. They knew plenty of processes and reports needed improvement and anticipated that their network of ambassadors could handle both. 'Get the process (that created the data) right, then lock in the gains' was the thinking.

AlOwaish asked members of Gulf Bank's Management Committee (MC) to nominate ambassadors. She advised the MC that her plan was, 'Let's get the people right first, then worry about technology.' Her original goal was 40 people, but the MC nominated over 140! Terrific news, but it meant her small team had to support three times as many people!

By mid-year, AlOwaish was both excited and nervous. She had ambassadors, a five-course curriculum under development, and was attracting good people to her team. But would it all come together? Her confidence received a big boost about an hour into the first training session! Ambassadors, many of whom had been openly sceptical, warmed up immediately to the ideas she and her team presented. They accepted and completed 'back-on-the-job' assignments given to build momentum. The second assignment called for ambassadors to lead their business groups in making a data quality measurement (since Kuwaitis work Sunday through Thursday, the Friday Afternoon Measurement is called the

'Thursday Morning Measurement' in Kuwait) and enabled AlOwaish's team to establish a powerful baseline and energize improvement across the company.

AlOwaish and her team communicated constantly and through a variety of means. They created a logo for the data ambassadors programme, and gave ambassadors branded notebooks and other memorabilia. They aimed to make the work fun, keeping everyone involved fully engaged.

Quite naturally, Gulf Bank's data programme had challenges starting up. But it also gained powerful supporters. Salma AlHajjaj, Head of Human Resources, assisted in dozens of ways and Dari AlBader, Head of Corporate Affairs, helped AlOwaish's team convey their messages powerfully. CEO Antoine Daher made timely appearances to convey his support. Finally, Menon, her boss, worked behind the scenes to secure resources and champion data and data quality.

There were other problems as well – most notably Covid. AlOwaish and her team adapted as needed. They read, learned and displayed the courage to try new things. Most importantly, they admitted they too were beginners. But their enthusiasm was contagious!

On her one-year anniversary, AlOwaish readily admitted that Gulf Bank's data journey had just begun. While the basics were coming together, 'data' was hardly mainstream, the cultural transformation was in the early stages, and the work to empower Gulf Bank strategies with data had not yet begun. And the difficult work of common language was on the critical path to some of those strategies. Still, they had traction. Senior leadership was beginning to buy in, a data team was focussed and on track, and the network of ambassadors was coming together. Everyone involved could rightly feel good about their efforts.

I find Gulf Bank's experiences instructive for companies and government agencies of all sizes. Enormous companies and government agencies may complain that Gulf Bank is too small and smallish companies that Gulf Bank is too large to hold relevant lessons for them. For data programmes must be built up, to embrace regular people. If your company is small, you may need a smaller data team and at most a few embedded data managers. If your company is large, you may need data teams in each business unit, with a corporate office coordinating them. But the work and relationships are recursive, meaning they scale up and down as needed.

Most important takeaways

- Five factors help define the composition and positioning of the core data teams companies need now:
  - getting the work done (from day-in, day-out data management to quality, to managing data science teams)
  - getting everyone involved, training people in their new responsibilities, and helping transform the company
  - data is a team sport, meaning the establishment and ongoing performance of data supply chains, common language, the data science bridge and change management
  - business priorities. aligning data and business priorities is essential
  - empowerment and fun
- Just like football, data is a team sport. In the analogy:
  - regular people are the players
  - senior leaders are owners and general managers
  - data teams are the coaches and assistant coaches
  - embedded data managers are the on-field captains
- Small, close-to-the-action, specialized data teams work best.
- Embedded data managers extend data teams.

Notes

1 R Bean and T Davenport. Are you asking too much of your chief data officer?, *Harvard Business Review*, 7 February 2020, hbr.org/2020/02/are-you-asking-too-much-of-your-chief-data-officer (archived at https://perma.cc/N2LL-X63J)

2 T Davenport and K Malone. Deployment as a critical business data science discipline, *Harvard Data Science Review*, 3.1, 10 February 2021, hdsr.mitpress.mit.edu/pub/2fu65ujf/release/2 (archived at https://perma.cc/VH3M-8KHR)

3 TC Redman. Your data initiatives can't just be for data scientists, *Harvard Business Review*, 22 March 2022, hbr.org/2022/03/your-data-initiatives-cant-just-be-for-data-scientists (archived at https://perma.cc/768S-2Y5X)

Conclusion

Courage required

An information technology cluster is not sufficient

To conclude, I'll put data and the recommendations here in historical perspective. In his study of economic disruption, Joseph Schumpeter noticed that technologies arrived in 'clusters'.[1] Thus, with electrification came dynamos, generators, switch gears and power distribution systems; with the automobile came production lines, road systems, oil refineries and traffic control. The cluster of information technologies over the past generation is impressive indeed: enormous increases in computing power, artificial intelligence, the cloud and blockchain, to name just a few.[2] But we're yet to see the enormous economic boost one might expect. Something is missing.[3,4,5,6]

I propose that high-quality, trusted data is the missing ingredient. We do not need great technologies if the data is poor – they just makes things worse! Conversely, data alone will not have the wide-scale impact that technology makes possible. Expressed differently, the 'I' is missing in the IT cluster.

By way of analogy, consider that an impressive technology cluster portends great opportunity for electric cars. But their widespread use is delayed because a critical component of the cluster – charging stations – is coming along much more slowly.[7]

So far, companies have placed far greater emphasis on technology than high-quality data and, if Schumpeter is right, sooner or later the two must go hand-in-hand. The situation is weirdly paradoxical. No one doubts that data is extremely valuable, maybe even more valuable than the technology. But technology garners the lion's share of attention. It is time for a better balance, a data AND information technology (D-IT) cluster, if you will.

Organizational innovation required

The second point is that organizational innovations are needed before the advantages of a technological cluster can come to fruition. Electrification provides a terrific example. Beforehand, factories were powered by a steam engine, with a system of pulleys powering the machines. The whole system was fraught, complex and elegant in its own way.

Electricity and electric motors, with their ability to power each machine separately, offered numerous advantages. But they required a redesign of the factories, and architects of the time knew nothing about electricity. It also presented a huge downside – mistakenly touching a live wire could prove fatal! It took 40 years of learning, experimentation and investment along multiple fronts to fully electrify the factory.[8] Those that could not make the needed changes suffered.

We are at a similar point with data. It's clear that data is powerful, but companies have not figured out how to put it to work. They cannot even consistently create high-quality data in one part of the company for use in a second. Further, bad data, misinformation and misguided analyses are dangerous. Until we build organizations better suited to data, the entire D-IT cluster will founder, holding companies back.

People to the fore

The third point is that the new cluster and people must figure out ways to accommodate each other. It is only natural that people (some of them anyway) resist new technologies. That resistance lessens as technologies become easier to use. Standard sockets and plugs certainly made electricity easier to use. In the best case, the technology becomes invisible. After just a bit of training and practice, most people don't even notice they are driving, most of the time anyway. And sometimes, people make most of the accommodations. For example, new factory workers coming off the farm had to shift the start of their workdays from the cock crowing to the factory whistle.

This is an important theme. Sooner or later the cluster must embrace everyone and large numbers of people must embrace the cluster. The central theme of this book is that this is yet to happen for data. The good news is that regular people enjoy data work!

THE PRINTING PRESS AND INFORMATION

A better analogy might involve the printing press, perhaps the most important information technology of the last 2,000 years. The Gutenberg press garners the most attention, but other technologies, such as those used to make cheap paper and ink, were essential to the cluster.

But that is just the beginning of the story. For when the printing press was invented, the Classics and Scripture dominated the book scene. It took nearly two generations for new topics (such as Machiavelli's *The Prince*) to appear, enhancing the cluster. Similarly, it took two generations for a publishing industry to emerge, bringing with it the needed organizational innovations. The third element, increasing the number of people who can read, is largely complete in much of the world.

The parallels to today are striking! Today's information technologies are impressive indeed. It is now time to focus on what comes next – high-quality data, better organizations for data, and regular people.

A jarring road ahead

I've done all I can to diagnose the issues, which include a lack of fully engaged people at all levels, silos that get in the way, general confusion about the separate and overlapping roles of data and technology, the lack of true data sharing, leadership on the side-lines, and cultures that purport to value data but do not. I've also done my best to propose the innovations and solutions needed to resolve these issues.

To be clear, these are organizational issues that must be solved by people, managers and leaders, NOT technology.

As I've already noted, implementing these innovations will not prove easy. Like those associated with previous technology clusters, making them will require considerable experimentation, learning and investment. They will prove incredibly disruptive and there will be plenty of failures.

I've also already noted that 'the business factory' actively resists the new ideas coming from the 'data science lab'. Companies prize stability and predictability. They may be happy to make small changes, but not the big innovations called for here. Consider the twin notions that regular people belong at the centre of the organization chart and that companies should see data as human empowerment. Those comfortable with command-and-control hierarchies will immediately object that this is all backwards: companies employ people to meet the company's needs, not to empower them. Only the enlightened will see that when it comes to data, human empowerment and company success go hand-in-hand. So, I expect these ideas will meet considerable resistance.

Resistance strikes me as particularly odd for several of the main ideas here. Consider the notion that regular people are both 'data creators' and 'data customers'. I just don't see anything controversial. It is observably true that all (the vast majority) serve in these capacities. Is it unreasonable to propose that they become good creators and customers? Similarly, it is observably true that data flows in complex ways across a company. Is it unreasonable to *manage* these data supply chains, particularly in light of how successful supply chain management for physical goods has proven?

Still I expect resistance, much in the form of delay. After all, it is all too easy to regard the next product launch, reorganization, regulatory demand or acquisition as more important than data. On and on. Forever.

If history provides any guidance, over the long haul, delay and resistance are futile. Even if your company leads your industry now, sooner or later some competitor or new entrant will fully embrace data, make these changes, and earn a measure of competitive advantage. It is the rock-solid certainty that those who don't keep up with the times, suffer!

Exacerbating this resistance is fear. I've never heard anyone say, 'I'm afraid' in a business setting, but you can hear it in the tone of people's voices, see it in their eyes, and feel it in their obfuscations. Frankly, I think most people and companies are smart to be afraid. Change is coming and adapting your management system to take advantage of data will prove very disruptive.

Which brings me back to courage. Fortunately, change also breeds opportunity and quite possibly rich rewards, for those courageous enough to seek and pursue it. More than anything else, unlocking the potential in data takes courage.

So we end where we began. With people!

Audaces fortuna juvet.
Fortune favours the brave.

Notes

1 This chapter makes use of the following (see also notes 2–6): WB Arthur. Is the information revolution dead?, E-Business Forum 2.0, March 2002, www. ebusinessforum.gr/old/content/downloads/IstheInformationRevolutionDead (archived at https://perma.cc/R57Z-9FSG)

2 JP Barlow. Cybernomics: Towards a theory of information economy (nd), The Merrill Lynch Forum, epdf.pub/cybernomics-toward-a-theory-of-information-economy.html (archived at https://perma.cc/7JKK-X8XK)

3 PF Drucker. The Next Information Revolution (nd), www.s-jtech.com/Peter%20 Drucker%20-%20the%20Next%20Information%20Revolution.pdf (archived at https://perma.cc/RED7-SQMQ)

4 M Hobart and Z Schiffman (1998) *Information Ages Literacy, Numeracy, and the Computer Revolution*, The Johns Hopkins University Press

5 C Freeman and F Louçã (2001) *As Time Goes By From the Industrial Revolutions to the Information Revolution*, Oxford University Press

6 A Chandler and J Cortada (eds) (2000) *A Nation Transformed by Information. How information has shaped the United States from colonial times to the present*, Oxford University Press

7 *The Economist*. Charging electric vehicles: Current situation, 11 December 2021, 55–58

8 Another example from an earlier time – it took nearly two generations after Guttenberg invented the printing press for a publishing industry, with authors writing about things other than Scripture, to emerge

RESOURCE CENTRE 1: TOOLKIT

Selected tools: 'How-tos' to help you get started

Contents

Tool A: Force field analysis: How to conduct
a force field analysis

Force field analysis (FFA) is a powerful tool that allows individuals and organizations to visualize its current situation in complex, multi-factor settings. Current state reflects a balance of *driving forces*, which help produce the desired results, and *restraining forces*, which contribute to poor results. FFA provides a means to sort this out and, more importantly, helps guide decision-making. If you want things to improve, you have three choices:

• you can strengthen and/or increase driving forces

• you can weaken and/or decrease restraining forces

• you can transform a restraining force into a driving force

This tool shows you how to create your own force field analysis using a problem set and analysis from my recent research.

Step 1: Specify your topic of interest

Draw a horizontal line across the centre of a sheet of paper or white-board (you can also use a downloadable file provided by *Sloan Management Review*).[1] This line will represent your topic of interest. Label the area above the line *restraining forces* and the area below the line *driving forces*.

From there, add five lines above and five lines below the topic of interest line. These markers will help represent the *strengths* of the restraining and driving forces (Figure A.1).

Next is defining the topic of interest. In this example, I've used 'the business impact of data science'. Note that FFA is quite flexible and can work for a range of technical, organizational and social topics.

Step 2: Brainstorm the driving and restraining forces

Driving forces go below the centre line and push up in favour of our selected topic. Restraining forces go above the centre line, and push down, holding back progress on the topic of interest.

FIGURE A.1 Impact of data science (1)

It is also helpful to think about the relative strength of each force. In this example, I'm using a scale of 1–5 (1 being weakest, 5 being strongest).

In Figure A.2, I've illustrated this point using one driving and restraining force each.

Developing a FFA is a great team exercise. Think broadly and get as many inputs as you can.

It's often useful to call out major subcategories of your topic first and then drill down to relevant individual forces. In this example, we searched for forces relevant to the impact of data science in six broad categories: external factors, data quality, data monetization, internal organizational factors, technology and defence.

Figure A.3 represents several weeks of iterative work. The notion that there might be built-in conflict between the data lab and factory initially struck my research team as counter-intuitive and we did not include it in early drafts. But as we talked to other experts, they all concurred; thus, it's reflected in the analysis.

FIGURE A.2 Impact of data science (2)

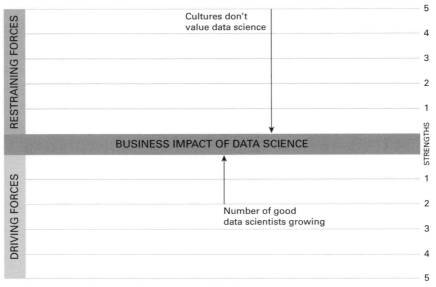

Step 3: Refine groupings and presentation of forces

Once you have determined all of the different forces to visualize and plotted them accordingly, organize and refine the graphic (Figure A.4). For example, you may wish to:

a simplify the graphic by grouping like items together; in our example, external factors, organization and data/technology proved useful groups

b align forces that work in direct opposition; in the example, we map opposing forces related to data quality

Note that the factors impacting the business value of data science are many and varied. One can feel quite good about recent developments: there certainly are far more data scientists, and more data and processing capability than ever before. But there is also a powerful array of restraining forces, especially the lack of a data culture in many organizations.

The project is now complete, though of course, you should take the next step, sorting out what to do with the results.

FIGURE A.3 Impact of data science (3)

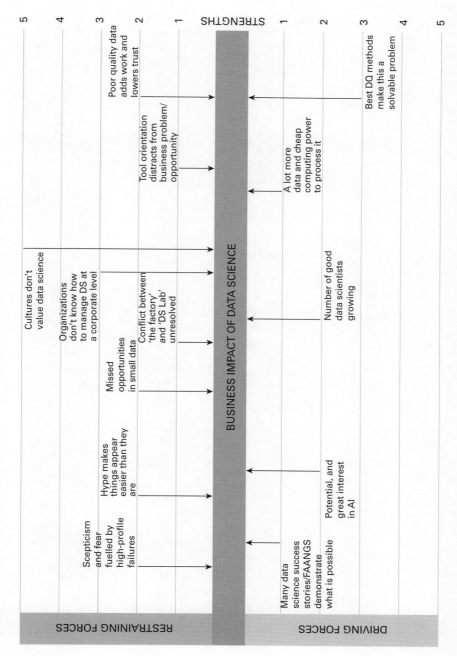

FIGURE A.4 Impact of data science (4)

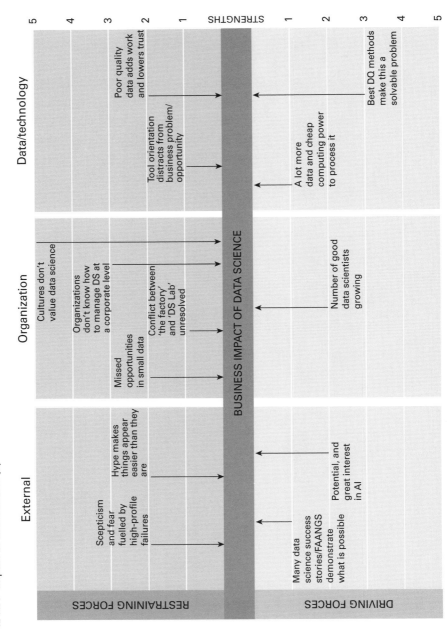

Step 4: Develop (then execute) a plan to improve progress

To effect change, your plan must strengthen and increase driving forces, weaken and decrease restraining forces, and/or transform restraining forces into driving forces:

- For driving forces, ask what your team/company can do to increase the power and effectiveness of each and push to develop ideas for new driving forces.

- To address restraining forces, ask what your organization can do to mitigate existing forces and prevent new opposing forces from forming.

- Similar to information gathering during the FFA process, your planning stage will benefit from casting a wide net. Make it a team exercise where you can benefit from a variety of different inputs and perspectives.

Tool B: Customer needs analysis: How to become a good data customer

I've stressed the roles of regular people in becoming good data customers. You can start doing so yourself, even better, with your team by following this four-step process.

Step 1: Sort out 'what we really need to know'

The question demands careful thought, but often people get caught up in making do with what they have and don't even think to ask. Start by brainstorming. Assemble people in a room (virtually if necessary), put the question to them, and record results on a big board, visible to all. I find that groups most often develop long lists – 50 or more needs.

The next part of the exercise is winnowing down the list to about a dozen most essential items. You can achieve this by progressively eliminating lower priority items. To complete the exercise, summarize your 'most important needs to know' very clearly. Go into depth here. For example, during the pandemic, public health leaders needed to know not just how many people died of Covid, but also *death rate, by age and current health*.

Step 2: Make sure the language associated with those needs is crystal clear

For example, a healthcare worker may need to know the *death rate due to coronavirus*. Thus, they must decide what exactly counts as a death due to coronavirus. Is the 37 year old, who experienced coronavirus-like symptoms, then self-quarantined and died at home, but never received a test, counted? How about the 93 year old, already battling advanced cancer, who dies after testing positive? There are many such details.

Step 3: Document the results of the first two steps and share them broadly

and

Step 4: Compare 'what we need to know' with 'what we actually know' and work to close the gaps

Work item by item, being as honest as you possibly can be. Work with existing data creators and sources to see if they can address gaps. If not, find new sources.

Tool C: The Friday Afternoon Measurement: How to baseline data quality[2]

The Friday Afternoon Measurement (FAM) helps people measure the quality of data they use, develop a high-level estimate of its impact, and synthesize the results. It is fungible, meaning it adapts itself well to different companies, processes and sets of data. Complete the following steps.

Step 1: Assemble the records

Assemble the last 100 data records you and/or your team used or created. For example, if your group takes customer orders, assemble the last 100 orders; if you create engineering drawings, assemble the last 100 drawings. Then focus on 10–15 critical data elements (or attributes) within the data record. Lay these out on a spreadsheet or on large sheets of paper.

Step 2: Set up a meeting

Ask two or three people with knowledge of the data to join you for a two-hour meeting. (The FAM takes its name because many people set up these meetings on Friday afternoon, when the pace of work slows.)

Step 3: Rate the data

Working record by record, mark obvious errors in red. For most records, this will go incredibly quickly. Your team members will either spot errors – the misspelled customer name or information that's been placed in the wrong column – or they won't. In some cases you'll engage in spirited discussions about whether an item is truly incorrect, but usually you will spend no more than 30 seconds on a record.

Step 4: Summarize the results

First, add a 'record perfect or not' column to your spreadsheet. Mark it 'yes' if there aren't any errors and 'no' if red appears in the record.

FIGURE C.1   Friday Afternoon Measurement summary sheet at Upscale Sweater

Data collected on 1 April 2023					
Indicator	Name	Size	Colour	Amount	Record perfect? (y/n)
Record A	Jane Doe	null	light blue	$129.00	n
B	John Smith	Med	blue	$129.00	y
C	Stuart Madnick	XXXL	red	$129.00	n
CV (100)	Alyson Heller	Med	blue	$129.00	
Error Count	0	24	5	2	perfect = 67

Count the number of perfect records and the number of errors in each column. You'll produce a table that looks much like Figure C.1.

Step 5: Interpret the results

Based on the analysis, the 'number of perfect records' is as follows: of the last 100 data records our group completed, we only completed two-thirds – 67 out of 100 – properly. Almost everyone will recognize this as poor performance indeed.

This finding confirms you have a data quality problem and you can, if you wish, stop here. But you can go further.

Step 6: Apply the Rule of Ten

The Rule of Ten is a rule of thumb that states, 'It costs 10 times as much to complete a unit of work when the input data is defective as it does when it is perfect.' Thus, in the example above, someone using the data will be able to do so without added effort two-thirds of the time, but one-third of the time it will cost about 10 times as much to make corrections and to complete the work.

As a simple example, suppose your work team must complete 100 units per day and each unit costs $1.00 when the data is perfect. If everything is perfect, a day's work costs $100 (100 units at $1.00 each). But with only 67 perfects:

Total cost = (67 × $1.00) + (33 × $1.00 × 10) = $67 + $330 = $397

As you can see, the total cost is almost *four times* as much as if the data was all good. Think of the difference as the cost of poor data quality. Most companies can't, and shouldn't, tolerate such costs.

Step 7: Make improvements

Now that you know you have a data problem and know the costs associated with it, you may wish to make some actual improvements! The spreadsheet indicates which attributes have errors, and by look-ing at that data you can see which attributes need fixing first. Tally the number of errors in each column, and focus on two to three attributes that have the highest totals. Find and eliminate their root causes. In most cases you should expect those responsible for creat-ing the data (either your team or another, depending on the data you selected) to make these improvements as part of their day-in, day-out jobs, with little to no capital investment. But you'll see the error rate decline and the associated costs diminish significantly.

Tool D: How to complete a small data science project[3]

Practically anyone can follow the data science process of Chapter 6 by themselves or, even better, with their teams. Completing one project will open your eyes to the millions of small data opportunities and enable you to work a bit more effectively with data scientists. (As we work through the steps here, I'll also point out important concepts in data science – from understanding variation to visualization.)

Step 1: Understand the problem/formulate goals

Start with something that interests, even bothers you, like consistently late-starting meetings. Whatever it is, form it up as a question and write it down: 'Meetings always seem to start late. Is that really true?'

Step 2: Collect data

Next, think through the data that can help answer your question and develop a plan for creating it. Write down all the relevant definitions and your protocol for collecting the data. For this particular example, you have to define when the meeting actually begins. Is it the time someone says 'Okay, let's begin'? Or the time the real business of the meeting starts? Does 'kibitzing' count?

Now collect the data. It is critical that you trust the data and, as you go, you're almost certain to find gaps in data collection. You may find that even though a meeting has started, it starts anew when a more senior person joins in. Modify your definition and protocol as you go along.

Step 3: Analyse the data

Sooner than you think, you'll be ready to start drawing some pictures. Good pictures make it easier for you to both understand the data and communicate main points to others. There are plenty of good tools to help, but I like to draw my first picture by hand. My go-to plot is a time–series plot, where the horizontal axis has the date and time, and the vertical axis the variable of interest. Thus, a point on the graph in Figure D.1 is the date and time of a meeting versus the number of minutes late.

Now return to the question that you started with and develop summary statistics. Have you discovered an answer? In this case, 'Over a two-week period, 10 per cent of the meetings I attended started on time. And, on average they started 12 minutes late.'

Don't stop there. Answer the 'so-what?' question. In this case, 'If those two weeks are typical, I waste an hour a day. And that costs the company $X/year. And frankly, that is time that I would rather spend at home with my family.'

Many analyses end because there is no 'so what?' Certainly, if 80 per cent of meetings start within a few minutes of their scheduled start times, the answer to the original question is 'No, meetings start pretty much on time' and there is no need to go further.

But this case demands more, as some analyses do. Get a feel for variation. Understanding variation leads to a better feel for the overall problem, deeper insights and novel ideas for improvement. Note on the picture that 8–20 minutes late is typical. A few meetings start right on time, others nearly a full 30 minutes late. It might be better if one could judge, 'I can get to meetings 10 minutes late, just in time for them to start', but the variation is too great.

Now ask, 'What else does the data reveal?' It strikes me that five meetings began exactly on time, while every other meeting began at least seven minutes late. In this case, bringing meeting notes to bear reveals that all five meetings were called by the Vice President of Finance, who evidently starts all meetings on time.

Step 4: Formulate findings/present results

and

Step 5: Put findings to work and support them

So where do you go from here? Are there important next steps? This example illustrates a common dichotomy. On a personal level, results

FIGURE D.1 Plot of meeting data

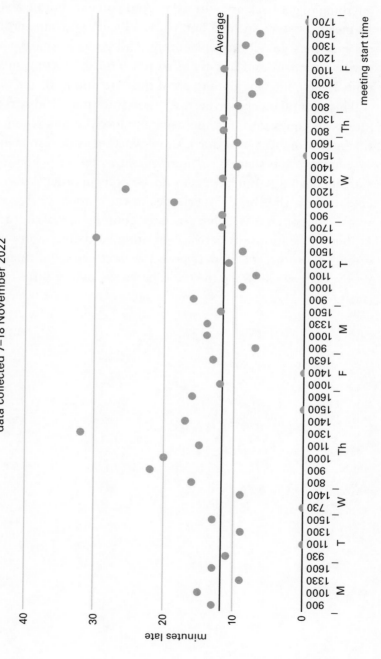

Do meetings start on time?

data collected 7–18 November 2022

pass both the 'interesting' and 'important' test. Most of us would give anything to get back an hour a day. And you may not be able to make all meetings start on time but, if the VP can, you can certainly start the meetings you control promptly. And you can share your results with your team and ask them to join you in starting meetings on time. Keep collecting data to see if they are doing so.

This completes the project. At the same time, it also raises more interesting questions. On the company level, results so far only pass the interesting test. You don't know whether your results are typical, or whether others can be as hard-nosed as the VP when it comes to starting meetings. But a deeper look is surely in order. Are your results consistent with others' experiences in the company? Are some days worse than others? Which starts later, conference calls or face to face? Is there a relationship between meeting start time and most senior attendee? Return to Step 1, pose the next group of questions, and repeat the process. Keep the focus narrow – two or three questions at most.

Tool E: Traits of great decision-makers: How to become a better decision-maker[4]

Healthy people follow certain habits: they eat right, get plenty of exercise, don't smoke, and so forth. Similarly, great decision-makers follow certain habits. You can become a better decision-maker by rating yourself against these habits and learning to follow a new one.

Step 1: Baseline your decision-making capabilities

Work through the list below, giving yourself a point for every habit you consistently demonstrate and half a point for those you follow most – but not all – of the time. Be hard on yourself. If you can only cite an instance or two, don't give yourself any credit.

	Score
I push decisions down to the lowest possible level.	
I bring as much diverse data and as many diverse viewpoints to any situation as I possibly can.	
I use data to develop a deeper understanding of the business context and the problem at hand.	
I develop an appreciation for variation.	
I deal reasonably well with uncertainty.	
I integrate my understanding of the data and its implications with my intuition.	
I recognize the importance of high-quality data and invest to make improvements.	
I conduct good experiments and research to supplement existing data and address new questions.	
I recognize that decision criteria can vary with circumstances.	
I realize that making a decision is only the first step – we must execute it. And I revise decisions as new data comes to light.	
I work to learn new skills and bring new data and new data technologies into my organization.	

(Continued)

(Continued)

I learn from my mistakes and help others do so.	
I strive to be a role model when it comes to data, working with leaders, peers and subordinates to help them become data-driven.	
Total points	

Step 2: Make a plan to improve

No matter how you score, it is important to get better. So set a goal of incorporating a new habit or two into your decision-making every year. Take this test every six months to make sure that you're on track.

Step 3: Recognize and act on a crisis

If you score fewer than 7 points, it's imperative that you move even faster. Target those behaviours where you gave yourself partial credit first and work hard to fully embed those habits into your daily work. Then build on your success to target areas where you were unable to give yourself any credit.

It may help to work with a colleague or your entire team on this exercise. You can improve together.

Tool F: How to set up and manage data supply chains[5]

The data supply chain management cycle is presented in Figure F.1. In my role as an advisor, I have found it unmatched at helping companies sort out and improve complex flows of data. It stems from methods used to manage physical supply chains. Brief descriptions of each step follow.

Step 1: Establish management responsibilities

First, name a 'data supply chain manager' and recruit a management team from each relevant department, including external data sources across the supply chain. Embedded data managers are great candidates. Next, put issues associated with data sharing and ownership front and centre. Most issues melt away, as few managers wish to take a hard stance against data sharing in front of their peers.

Step 2: Understand customers and their needs

Identify and document the data and associated cost, time and quality requirements needed to create and maintain data products.

FIGURE F.1 The data supply chain management cycle

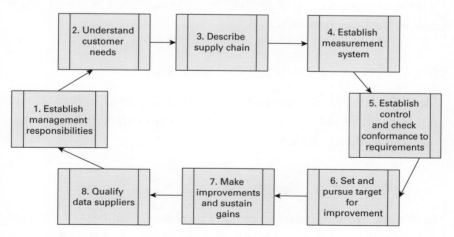

Step 3: Describe the supply chain

Develop a flowchart that describes points of data creation/original sources of data and the steps taken to move, enrich and analyse data for use in data products.

Step 4: Establish measurement system

Generally, the idea is to implement measurements that indicate whether requirements are met. Start with data accuracy and the elapsed time from data creation to incorporation into a data product. Measures will vary for each data product's supply chain.

Step 5: Establish process control and assess conformance to requirements

Use the measurements of Step 4 to put the process in control and determine how well the requirements of Step 2 are met and to identify gaps.

Step 6: Set and pursue targets for improvement

Set targets that close the gaps between customer requirements and current performance. Investigate the supply chain to identify needed improvements and determine where gaps uncovered in Step 5 originate in the flowchart of Step 3.

Step 7: Make improvements and sustain the gains

Identify and eliminate root causes of gaps identified in Step 6, and return to previous steps if necessary. Once eliminated, make sure that root causes do not return.

Step 8: 'Qualify' data suppliers

Companies will continue to employ increasing numbers of external data suppliers and it is helpful to identify those that consistently provide high-quality data. Audits of their data quality programmes provide the means to 'qualify' those that do and identify areas of weakness in those that do not.

Tool G: How to manage data science at the enterprise level[6]

As presented in Figure G.1, data science must be managed as a cycle, or continuous loop. It resides within the context of the organization and its overall business strategy. That strategy determines *what* needs to be accomplished and provides high-level direction to the data science bridge. Elements of this direction can be quite broad, including desired competitive position, financial goals, opportunities to innovate within the 'lab', and specific 'factory' improvement targets. Data science projects are then implemented and managed. The results – successes, of course, but failures, too – feed back into the business's overall context and should inform business strategy. This completes the cycle.

The process itself recognizes five core tasks or subprocesses:

Task 1: Drive collaboration across the organization as it relates to data science

Most companies should start with this task. Data science is a team sport, and without teamwork, mediocre results are all but assured.

FIGURE G.1 The data science management process and its business context

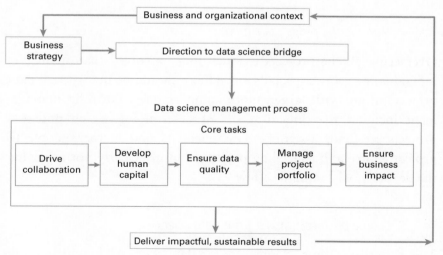

Task 2: Develop the human capital required to achieve the organization's data science objectives

Importantly, this includes data scientists and regular people in their roles as small data scientists and contributors to larger efforts.

Task 3: Ensure data quality

Most data science teams are aware of the importance of data quality and devote a substantial fraction of their effort to dealing with mundane quality issues. Yet data scientists are organizationally separate from data creation, so they are not in a good position to evaluate quality, much less improve it. Complicating matters further, as models are turned over to the factory, quality issues expand from the historical data used to train the model to the newly created data used to operate it.

The data science bridge must help sort all this out. It must help build the data supply chains to ensure that managerial accountability for data quality is clear in both model development and in production; that quality standards, policies, procedures, and tools are in place; and that data scientists, external data providers and employees follow them.

Task 4: Manage the project portfolio

Overseeing all the projects is much more involved than managing individual projects, especially since there should be many small data projects along with larger, more complex ones. Portfolio management includes the difficult tasks of determining which potential projects to fund, assigning data scientists and factory people to project teams, and cancelling projects that are clearly not achieving the desired goals, to name a few.

Task 5: Ensure business impact from data science

This subprocess aims to integrate the data science lab, which develops the technology, with the factory, which deploys the technology.

Tool H: How to evaluate whether you can successfully develop and promulgate common language

It takes a lot to successfully develop and promulgate a common language. Those leading the effort should critically evaluate their organization against the following criteria.[7]

Sense of urgency

1 *Sense of urgency*: employees at all levels must be able to explain why common language is needed.

Long-term thinking

2 *Vision:* a clear statement/picture of the intended reality and the benefits that new reality will convey.
3 *Clarity of purpose/shared business objective:* long-term business objectives must be clearly stated and agreed.

People, process and structure

The following are needed:

4 *A very senior responsible manager* (e.g. a Head of Common Language): with the authority, gravitas and level to articulate/sell the business case, set direction, remove obstacles, provide resources, align others and enlist others to contribute.
5 *Relentless change leaders:* who introduce the need for common language, persistently advocate and fight for it, define the business case and the vision, convert others, build a strong partnership between all involved, provide a means to implement common language, and deliver the business benefits promised.
6 *A well-defined process:* to get the right people involved and manage the work described in Figure H.1.

7 *Skilled staff:* needed roles include:

   a. *data modellers,* who can clarify underlying concepts that form the foundations of common language

   b. *data definers,* who can write clear definitions

   c. *responsible managers,* who represent the interests of their departments AND are also able to collaborate to achieve win–win to meet the needs of the enterprise

   d. *process managers,* who are responsible for coordinating the work

   e. *enforcers,* who ensure that the common vocabulary is adhered to, particularly in databases, computer systems and applications

   f. *communicators,* who can communicate the concepts to the rest of the organization, vendors, etc

8 *IT and all the business departments must contribute:* each must name a *responsible manager,* who has the authority to speak for and represent the needs of his/her department.

Adoption and growth

9 *Adoption:* the common language must be built into the day-to-day vocabulary of the organization, its work processes and its data architecture. It must be adhered to in the development and purchase of new systems and applications.

10 *Growth:* the organization must have the capacity to include new concepts and/or terms, as the business grows and changes, and to eliminate those that no longer matter.

FIGURE H.1 Developing and promulgating common language[8]

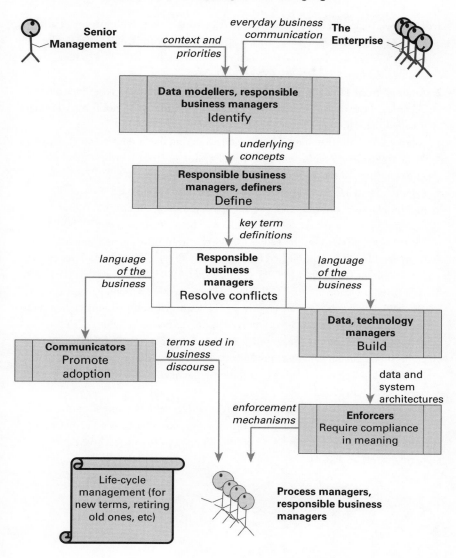

Notes

1 This tool is adapted from TC Redman. Visualizing change with force-field analysis, *Sloan Management Review*, 2 August 2021. For the promised downloadable toolkit see: sloanreview.mit.edu/wp-content/uploads/2021/07/79d426806a-2.pdf (archived at https://perma.cc/6LYQ-GKQJ)

2 Adapted from TC Redman (2016) *Getting in front on data: Who does what*, Technics. Note that in some parts of the world 'Friday Afternoon Measurement' is called the 'Thursday Morning Measurement'

3 Adapted from TC Redman. How to start thinking like a data scientist, *Harvard Business Review*, 29 November 2013, blogs.hbr.org/2013/11/how-to-start-thinking-like-a-data-scientist/ (archived at https://perma.cc/GWG7-5544)

4 Adapted from TC Redman. Are you data-driven? Take a hard look in the mirror, *Harvard Business Review*, 11 July 2013, blogs.hbr.org/2013/07/are-you-data-driven-take-a-har/ (archived at https://perma.cc/UX5S-NSE4)

5 This section is based on the Process Quality and Improvement Guidelines developed by AT&T, published by Dontech as *Process Quality Management & Improvement Guidelines (AT&T Quality Library)* (1998) by Roger Ackerman

6 RW Hoerl, D Kuonen and TC Redman. The data science management process, *Sloan Management Review*, 12 July 2021, sloanreview.mit.edu/article/the-data-science-management-process/ (archived at https://perma.cc/DH4F-TSYN)

7 D Hay, T Redman, CL Yonke and J Zachman. Developing and adopting a common language: What's required from an organizational perspective, tdan.com/developing-and-adopting-a-common-language/26284 (archived at https://perma.cc/L3G6-ZCAD)

8 D Hay, T Redman, CL Yonke and J Zachman. Developing and adopting a common language: What's required from an organizational perspective, tdan.com/developing-and-adopting-a-common-language/26284 (archived at https://perma.cc/H2TS-PSC4)

RESOURCE CENTRE 2: CURRICULUM FOR TRAINING REGULAR PEOPLE

As laid out fully in Chapter 3, sooner or later regular people should bear five specific responsibilities for data:

1 as *customers* and *creators* in **quality programmes**

2 as *small data scientists* in **process improvement**

3 as *collaborators, customers* and *data creators* in **larger data science,** artificial intelligence, digital transformation and other monetization projects

4 as *guardians* of the company's data assets, especially in understanding and following **privacy** and **security** policy

5 as better **decision-makers**

This leads to the question, 'What knowledge and skills must they possess to have a reasonable shot at fulfilling those responsibilities?' This portion of the Resource Centre proposes syllabi for three courses that answer that question. Individuals can use it to sort out the training they need and companies can use it to develop their training programmes (please note that my company offers much of this training). It also makes several observations and offers some advice about delivering the training.

NOTE There is lots of material on many of these topics, some of it quite good. I've provided references to my relevant articles in the Notes because they were written with regular people specifically in mind.

DISCLAIMER The courses described here are not sufficient for full-time data professionals. Depending on their specific plans, companies may well need people with deep expertise in data quality, metadata management, privacy, security and data science.

First data course

The first course consists of seven 'skills' that are already important and will become increasingly so. I liken them to the basic reading skills that became important as the Industrial Age gained steam and to the basic computer skills that became increasingly important starting in the mid-1990s. These form the first course. Everyone needs them!

Upon completion, regular people and embedded data managers should be able to:

A: FOLLOW RELEVANT DATA POLICIES

1 Understand and follow company policies regarding data security, privacy, retention and destruction.

B: CONTRIBUTE TO DATA QUALITY IMPROVEMENT[1]

2 Understand what constitutes high-quality data, the importance of eliminating root causes of error, and their roles in such efforts:

  a. become a good data customer: sort out how they use data on the job and communicate requirements to data sources; work with data creators and sources to obtain high-quality data

  b. become a good data creator: understand customer needs and participate in quality improvement efforts

  c. use customer–supplier model to understand data flows and build relationships between data creators and customers

  d. develop a nose for bad data (e.g. not be fooled by 'continue straight' in the face of a 'bridge out' sign) – if something 'smells wrong', say something

3 Make a simple data quality measurement using the Friday Afternoon Measurement method (as in Tool C).[2,3]

C: APPLY DATA AND DATA SCIENCE ON THE JOB

4 Understand data and descriptive statistics in the context of their jobs:

a. what a datum is (NOTE: here I explicitly mean the singular of data)

b. what average and percentages are and why they are important

c. identify bold-faced attempts to 'lie with statistics' and/or make inferences that are unsupported by the data

5 Clearly articulate a (business) problem of interest, gather some basic data on that topic, make some simple statistical and graphical summaries, and draw conclusions.[4,5] 'Tasks' include:

a. defining a problem

b. defining some data that bears on that problem

c. setting up a means to collect that data

d. collecting that data

e. making a time–series plot

f. making a Pareto plot

g. calculating the average

h. drawing conclusions

i. asking follow-up questions (merges into the next skill)

6 Understand and apply the scientific method. Dig one level deeper into the data to:

a. develop a deeper understanding of 'what's really going on'[6]

b. search for a root cause; sometimes I call this, 'turn over a rock and see what crawls out'

c. smoke out results that are too good, or too bad, to be true[7]

7 Use data to tell a compelling story/paint a picture of something important in your work environment. Use appropriate graphics to highlight the main points.[8]

Second data course

The second course consists of seven skills that build on those of the first course. I would be hard pressed to argue that all employees need these skills immediately. But embedded data managers need them now and I anticipate demand for these skills will grow. People with these skills and companies with people who have them can do so much more.

Upon completion, regular people and embedded data managers should be able to:

D: LEAD DATA QUALITY WORK AT THE TEAM LEVEL

8 Lead a data quality improvement project and team.

9 Understand and use control charts, where appropriate. Define and implement other simple controls in the context of their team's work.

E: CONDUCT MORE ADVANCED DATA SCIENCE PROJECTS TO DEVELOP DEEPER INSIGHTS ON THE JOB

10 Understand and apply the distinction between correlation and cause and effect, and between the description of what happened and a prediction about what will happen.[9]

11 Understand variation and uncertainty and apply that understanding on the job.[10]

12 Understand the distinction between a description of 'what has happened' in contrast to a 'prediction about the future'. Make simple predictions and understand more complex ones.[11]

13 Understand regression analysis and how to apply regression on the job.[12]

F: BECOME A BETTER DECISION-MAKER BOTH INDIVIDUALLY AND AS A MEMBER OF A TEAM

14 Bring more data to the decisions you make alone and with others. Know how to combine 'the data' with intuitions where the data leaves off. Strive to make data-driven decisions.[13,14,15]

Third data course

The third course builds on the first two.

Upon completion, attendees should be able to:

G: UTILIZE MORE ADVANCED DATA SCIENCE

15 Work with data analysts, statisticians, data scientists and others to:

   a. implement more complex analyses and models into your team's work

   b. demand much from them, asking hard questions[16]

   c. know when they are over your head, avoid making claims that they are not qualified to make, and know how to seek expert help

16 Integrate new data with old and adjust plans and decisions as a result. (NOTE: This is what Bayesian statistics (e.g. Nate Silver) is all about.)

17 Not be fooled by more sophisticated attempts to lie with statistics, especially those that make things appear better or worse than they are.

18 Develop an appreciation for risk that embraces both uncertainty and magnitude of loss. Combine that appreciation with potential gains.

19 Know when a good experiment is called for and appreciate the concepts of 'control' and 'randomization' in such settings.[17]

20 Develop a deeper appreciation of the interactions of forces driving progress and holding it back using force field analysis (as in Tool A).

Deploying this training

Any manager scanning through the courses outlined above will remark, 'Oh my gosh, this is so extensive. How will we ever pull this off? Even afford it?'

My reactions. First, there is no sugar-coating the fact that deploying this training will take a long time and cost a lot of money. From my perspective, too many companies have underinvested in their people for too long. There is no denying that educating a workforce for any transformation, never mind one as fundamental as data, is expensive. So suck it up. Be smart about your investments, but don't underinvest in people. As a former boss used to say, 'If you consider the cost of education too high, consider the cost of ignorance.'

Over the years, I've advised on and participated in many data education programmes. I've learned a lot along the way. The following distils some major themes.

You should probably train embedded data managers and senior leaders first. Embeds have less fear of data (more below) and they are well placed to help others when their turn come. Training senior leaders is problematic, so starting early is essential. Another great place to start is with new employees. The aforementioned Gulf Bank includes a one-hour session on new employees' responsibilities as data customers and data creators as part of onboarding. Not only is this effective; it conveys the importance the company attaches to data from the very start.

Second, it is important to bear in mind that many people fear data. Indeed, some readily admit that 'statistics was my least favourite course in college' and/or that even the most basic analysis leaves them cold. You must do all you can to acknowledge and address this fear. In particular, the first course should be taught by the best instructors and, ideally, via in-person classes of no more than 25.

Third, most people learn best when they can see the relevancy of what they're being taught to their work or home life. So, all courses should feature relevant and 'on-the-job' examples in which attendees apply the main lessons. Use completed exercises to develop an ever larger body of examples. Further, people use Excel, Tableau and other tools on the job. This training should use such tools (though I am tool-agnostic).

Building on this point, myself (and many others) stand in awe of the beauty, power and joy in 'understanding the numbers', using data to learn more about the world, solve problems and contribute to larger efforts. I hope that as many people as possible get to see this beauty, use this power and feel this joy. So I'd like this instruction to convey the simplicity of the basic concepts, build confidence, and provide a 'go-to' reference people can use throughout their careers. Most of all, I want the training to be fun!

DATA LITERACY

I don't like the term 'data literacy'. Where I grew up 'illiterate' meant 'stupid' and I don't like that connotation applied to people who never had a chance to learn. Instead, I prefer the term 'data savvy', and it applies to both people and companies.

Finally, computer-based training. While great in-person training is best, it is expensive. Even more importantly, there are a limited number of qualified trainers. So computer-based training may be your only alternative. Owing to the importance of relevant examples, larger companies should consider commissioning training that features the best trainers and their companies' examples.

Notes

1   Full details on anything in this curriculum related to data quality can be found in TC Redman (2016) *Getting in Front on Data: Who Does What*, Technics. Though I didn't know it at the time, this book could also be titled, 'The Regular Person's Guide to Data Quality'

2   TC Redman. Assess whether you have a data quality problem, *Harvard Business Review*, 28 July 2016, hbr.org/2016/07/assess-whether-you-have-a-data-quality-problem (archived at https://perma.cc/D9W2-5R8S)

3   TC Redman. The Friday Afternoon Measurement [video], YouTube, www.youtube.com/watch?v=X8iacfMX1nw (archived at https://perma.cc/97EA-W4MQ)

4   TC Redman. How to start thinking like a data scientist, *Harvard Business Review*, 29 November 2013, blogs.hbr.org/2013/11/how-to-start-thinking-like-a-data-scientist/ (archived at https://perma.cc/5TKB-MJ8X)

5   RW Hoerl and D Kuonen. Framing data science problems the right way from the start, *Sloan Management Review*, 14 April 2022, sloanreview.mit.edu/article/framing-data-science-problems-the-right-way-from-the-start/ (archived at https://perma.cc/N4TE-YTHV)

6   TC Redman. Even the tiniest error can cost a company millions, *Harvard Business Review*, 7 August 2014, hbr.org/2014/08/even-the-tiniest-error-can-cost-a-company-millions (archived at https://perma.cc/77Q8-DAD8)

7   TC Redman. When it comes to data, scepticism matters, *Harvard Business Review*, 22 October 2014, hbr.org/2014/10/when-it-comes-to-data-skepticism-matters (archived at https://perma.cc/3J9Q-VWZE)

8   TC Redman. Data doesn't speak for itself, *Harvard Business Review*, 29 April 2014, hbr.org/2014/04/data-doesnt-speak-for-itself (archived at https://perma.cc/RG5X-YLDK)

9   TC Redman. How to explore cause and effect like a data scientist, *Harvard Business Review*, 19 February 2014, hbr.org/2014/02/how-to-explore-cause-and-effect-like-a-data-scientist (archived at https://perma.cc/6KTF-L7YW)

10 TC Redman. Do you understand the variance in your data?, *Harvard Business Review*, 16 August 2019, hbr.org/2019/08/do-you-understand-the-variance-in-your-data (archived at https://perma.cc/7FJC-U8UD)

11 TC Redman. Algorithms make better predictions – except when they don't, *Harvard Business Review*, 17 September 2014, hbr.org/2014/09/algorithms-make-better-predictions-except-when-they-dont (archived at https://perma.cc/4GZE-R2FD)

12 A Gallo. A refresher on regression analysis, *Harvard Business Review*, November 2015, hbr.org/2015/11/a-refresher-on-regression-analysis (archived at https://perma.cc/5VNW-NN96)

13 (See also notes 14 and 15) TC Redman. Are you data driven? Take a hard look in the mirror, *Harvard Business Review*, 11 July 2013, blogs.hbr.org/2013/07/are-you-data-driven-take-a-har/ (archived at https://perma.cc/P2AA-GB3N)

14 TC Redman. Become more data-driven by breaking these bad habits, *Harvard Business Review*, 12 August 2013, blogs.hbr.org/2013/08/becoming-data-driven-breaking/ (archived at https://perma.cc/E3UM-3YXJ)

15 TC Redman. Root out bias from your decision-making process, *Harvard Business Review*, 10 March 2017, hbr.org/2017/03/root-out-bias-from-your-decision-making-process (archived at https://perma.cc/8B6T-FDRA)

16 TC Redman and W Sweeney. Seven questions to ask your data geeks, *Harvard Business Review*, 10 June 2013, blogs.hbr.org/2013/06/seven-questions-to-ask-your-da/ (archived at https://perma.cc/5S2N-HTRW)

17 TC Redman. In a big data world, don't forget experimentation, *Harvard Business Review*, 8 May 2013, blogs.hbr.org/2013/05/in-a-big-data-world-dont-forge/ (archived at https://perma.cc/Q4GE-DNQK)

INDEX

The index is filed in alphabetical, word-by-word order. Numbers are filed as spelt out; acronyms and abbreviations are filed as presented. Page locators in italics denote information within a figure or table